Environmental Biology

Michael Reiss

Jenny Chapman

Series editor: Mary Jones

CAMBRIDGE
UNIVERSITY PRESS

PUBLISHED BY THE PRESS SYNDICATE OF THE UNIVERSITY OF CAMBRIDGE
The Pitt Building, Trumpington Street, Cambridge, United Kingdom

CAMBRIDGE UNIVERSITY PRESS
The Edinburgh Building, Cambridge CB2 2RU, UK   http://www.cup.cam.ac.uk
40 West 20th Street, New York, NY 10011-4211, USA   http://www.cup.org
10 Stamford Road, Oakleigh, Melbourne 3166, Australia
Ruiz de Alarcón 13, 28014 Madrid, Spain

© Cambridge University Press 2000

First published 2000

Printed in the United Kingdom at the University Press, Cambridge

Typeface Swift   *System* QuarkXPress®

A catalogue record for this book is available from the British Library

ISBN 0 521 78727 0 paperback

Produced by Gecko Ltd, Bicester, Oxon, UK

Front cover photographs: China clay tip, St Austell, UK (© Bob Gibbs/Woodfall Wild
Images); oil tanker wreck, Sleigh Head, Ireland (Telegraph Colour Library)

Contents

Introduction

Cambridge Advanced Sciences

The *Cambridge Advanced Sciences* series has been developed to meet the demands of all the new AS and A level science examinations. In particular, it has been endorsed by OCR as providing complete coverage of their specifications. The AS material is presented as a single text for each of biology, chemistry and physics. Material for the A2 year comprises six books in each subject: one of core material and one for each option. Some material has been drawn from the existing *Cambridge Modular Sciences* books; however, the majority is entirely new.

During the development of this series, the opportunity has been taken to improve the design, and a complete and thorough new writing and editing process has been applied. Much more material is now presented in colour. Although the existing *Cambridge Modular Sciences* texts do cover some of the new specifications, the *Cambridge Advanced Sciences* books cover every OCR learning objective in detail. They are the key to success in the new AS and A level examinations.

OCR is one of the three unitary awarding bodies offering the full range of academic and vocational qualifications in the UK. For full details of the new specifications, please contact OCR:

OCR
1 Hills Rd
Cambridge CB1 2EU
Tel: 01223 553311

Environmental Biology – an A2 option text

Environmental Biology contains everything needed to cover the A2 option of the same name. It combines entirely new text and illustrations with revised and updated material from *Ecology and Conservation*, previously available in the *Cambridge Modular Sciences* series. In a further improvement, *Environmental Biology* is in full colour, greatly enhancing its accessibility and usefulness.

The book is divided into seven chapters. Chapter 1 serves as an introduction to the subject whilst chapters 2–7 correspond to the modules Agriculture and the Environment, Pollution, Conservation of Resources, Conservation Issues (divided into UK and International) and Ecological Fieldwork.

Chapter 2 is entirely new, whilst all chapters reflect the new specification's shift in approach and the latest developments in this fast-changing subject.

In addition, a glossary of terms is included, linked to the main text via the index.

Authors' dedication
To Sally Corbet and Richenda Huxley

CHAPTER 1

Introduction to environmental biology

By the end of this chapter you should be able to:

1 explain the meanings of the terms *habitat*, *microhabitat*, *niche* and *population*;

2 distinguish between a *community* and an *ecosystem*;

3 describe similarities and differences between the growth in numbers of the human population and other animal populations;

4 outline the effects of human activity on the natural environment;

5 explain the value of monitoring the environment.

What is ecology?

This book is about ecology and conservation. **Ecology** is the study of organisms in their natural surroundings. The word ecology comes from two Greek words – *oikos* meaning home and *logos* meaning understanding. So ecology is all about understanding the homes of animals, plants and other organisms. The surroundings of an organism are known as its **environment**. Environments consist of many components including both *physical* features, such as climate and soil type, and *biological* features, such as predators and prey. The term **environmental biology** has wider connotations than ecology because it includes the study of humans in the environment, so you will find such subjects as agriculture, pollution and the unnatural surroundings we create in this book too.

Understanding the ecology of an area is like trying to put together a gigantic, multidimensional jigsaw. Some pieces are the individual species in the area. In an oak wood, for example (*figure 1.1*), the species might include bluebells, oak trees, earthworms, snails, hedgehogs, wood ants and tawny owls. Other pieces in the jigsaw are the important aspects of the physical environment, for example the pH of the rainwater, the total amount that falls in a year, how it is distributed throughout the seasons, and significant information about the temperature, sunlight and soil type. The jigsaw pieces interlock with one another in numerous, subtle ways.

In many ways ecology is a relatively new science. Indeed, the word was only coined by the German biologist Ernst Haeckel in 1869, fully ten years after Charles Darwin published his theory of

● **Figure 1.1** Stoneywell Wood, Leicestershire, in spring. The leaves on the oak trees are just emerging above the carpet of bluebells.

natural selection. Yet, in little over a century ecology has grown to become one of the most important disciplines within biology. Like all branches of science, it has its own language. This includes the terms habitat, population, community and ecosystem, which you will have already met in *Biology 1*.

A **habitat** is the place where an organism lives. The word is Latin and literally means 'it dwells'. Actually, organisms from a single species can live in a number of habitats. For example, the common rat (*Rattus norvegicus*) is typically found associated with farms, refuse tips, sewers and warehouses. However, it also occurs in hedgerows close to cereal crops or sugar beet, and in salt marshes. On islands (e.g. the Isle of Man, Rhum and Lundy) rats also occupy grassland and the sea shore.

With small organisms, especially those living in a restricted area such as in the soil or on a single plant or animal, it is worth being more precise about exactly where they live. The term **microhabitat** – 'a small habitat' – is used to describe this. A single habitat may have many microhabitats. For example, if you are an insect living on an oak tree, life is very different depending on whether you live on the upper surface of the leaves, the lower surface of the leaves or inside them. It is even more different if you live under the bark, next to the roots or inside an acorn. Each of these different places is a microhabitat.

A **niche** is a complete description of *how* the organism relates to its physical and biological environment. Just as in a jigsaw puzzle each piece has its own unique shape and pattern, and only fits in one place, so each species has a unique niche – the way it fits into its environment.

Consider a particular species, the grey heron (*Ardea cinerea*). Its habitats are water meadows, rivers, lakes and the sea shore. A complete account of its niche would include a description both of its physical environment (such as the type of water it needs, the temperature range in which it can survive and reproduce) and of its biological environment (such as the prey it eats, its competitors and the vegetation it needs for its nest).

It is difficult to provide a quantitative description of an organism's niche. *Figure 1.2* shows the feeding niche of the blue-grey gnatcatcher,

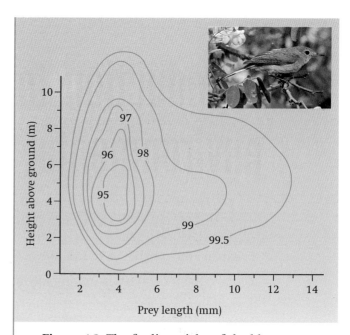

● **Figure 1.2** The feeding niche of the blue-grey gnatcatcher (*Polioptila caerulea*). The contours show the feeding frequencies for adult birds during the nesting period in July and August in oak woodlands in California. 95% of their diet is taken within the contour marked 95, 96% within the contour marked 96, and so on.

Polioptila caerulea, a North American bird. This is an **insectivore** and the horizontal axis shows the length of the insects on which it feeds. The vertical axis shows the height above ground at which it forages. The contour lines with numbers indicate the frequency with which the birds feed at a particular height and on a particular length of prey. You can see that the birds concentrate on prey 4 mm in length, which they catch about 3–6 m off the ground.

However, there are many other aspects to an organism's niche in addition to its feeding niche. In theory, other axes could be added at right-angles to those in *figure 1.2*. Temperature could be shown on a third axis, risk of predation at different times of the year on a fourth, height above ground of the bird's nest on a fifth, and so on. In practice, though, no more than two or three axes can be shown on a graph. Computers, however, can store and compute data for many more.

The ecological principle that each species has its own unique niche and that no two species can coexist if they occupy the same niche is known as **Gause's competitive exclusion principle**. The biologist G. F. Gause gets the credit because of his research on single-celled ciliates in the genus *Paramecium*.

A **population** is a group of individuals within a species that have the opportunity to breed with one another because they live in the same area at the same time. It follows from this definition that individuals from two different species cannot belong to the same population. This is because, with occasional exceptions, species are **reproductively isolated** from one another. Tawny owls do not breed with short-eared owls, for example.

Most species are divided into many populations that are geographically separated. Bluebells in one wood, for example, will belong to a different population from the bluebells in another wood several kilometres away. Indeed, in a large wood there may be several populations of bluebells, though the boundaries between populations may be somewhat arbitrary.

A **community** is an association of species that live together in some common environment or habitat. Most communities are composed of a mixture of prokaryotes, protoctists, fungi, plants and animals. The organisms in a community interact with one another in all sorts of ways. For a start, there will be feeding relationships. In most communities, **autotrophs** (also known as **producers** and comprising green plants, photosynthetic algae, photosynthetic bacteria and chemosynthetic bacteria) provide food for **herbivores** (also known as **primary consumers**). In turn, herbivores are eaten by **first-level carnivores** (also known as **secondary consumers**), and these may be eaten by **second-level carnivores** (or **tertiary consumers**). Eventually organisms die and their remains are broken down by **decomposers**. These feeding relationships can be represented by **food chains** or by **food webs** that show the interrelationships between the various food chains in a community.

The species in a community also interact with one another in other ways. They may rely on one another for reproduction, as is the case in insect-pollinated plants. Or one species may act as a home for another, as a humpback whale carries barnacles. Or the interaction may be more subtle – all the species in a woodland, for example, rely on the activities of the various soil organisms which recycle nutrients.

The term 'community' is a valuable one in ecology. However, in 1935 Sir Arthur Tansley invented the term **ecosystem** because he realised that the organisms that make up a community cannot realistically be considered independently of their physical environment. The term ecosystem, therefore, applies to a community of organisms and its associated physical environment.

There is one other feature of ecosystems and their associated communities worth stressing. This is that ecosystems are *dynamic*. Indeed, some ecosystems change as new species invade and others die out. A grassland invaded by shrubs and trees will change gradually as scrubland and then woodland develops. In a mature ecosystem, such as oak woodland, the population sizes and activities of the different species will alter from season to season and year to year. The bluebells in *figure 1.1* flower so beautifully in spring, but by late summer they have set seed, the leaves have died back and the bluebell bulbs are ready to lie dormant until the next spring.

SAQ 1.1

Arrange the following terms in a hierarchy of descending size and complexity: community, habitat, ecosystem, microhabitat.

SAQ 1.2

What parts of an ecosystem are also found in its community?

Humans in the environment

We have given ourselves a Latin binomial, *Homo sapiens*, just like all the other species we have classified. However, it is obvious that the impact humans have on the environment is unlike that of any other species. Ancient humans evolved in Africa and migrated out into Asia and Europe a million or more years ago. A second wave of migration of modern humans spread out of Africa about 130 000 years ago resulting in the colonisation of every continent.

Before humans evolved, of course, all the communities in the world were natural. In Britain,

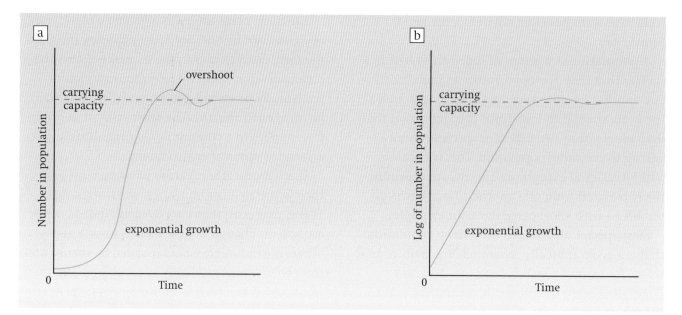

● **Figure 1.3** Population growth.   **a** Normal plot of population increasing exponentially until the carrying capacity is reached, when the population stabilises.   **b** A log-normal plot of the same data as **a**. With population plotted on a log scale an exponential curve is represented by a straight line.

natural vegetation during the Ice Ages was tree-less Arctic grassland called tundra; during warmer interglacials, after the ice sheets melted, trees invaded. In the south, forests of oaks, ash, lime and hornbeam grew; in the Scottish high-lands, the main vegetation was Scots pine conifer forest. These mature forests are called the **climax vegetation**, but such vegetation is now rare due to human activities.

Humans learned to make and use fire early in their history, about half a million years ago – very useful during Ice Ages! Before this, only lightning started wildfires that had the potential to damage vegetation. About 10 000 years ago humans also began to change the natural vegetation by cultivat-ing crops. Animals were domesticated at about the same time. Captive animals graze areas of vegeta-tion in much greater densities than natural animal populations do. The practice of burning and grazing led to the vegetation in many areas of the world developing into grasslands (see page 10). As human populations grew, their dwellings – in villages, towns and then cities – also restructured or even destroyed the vegetation.

As humans are animals, human population biology might be expected to follow the same rules as those of other animal populations (*figure 1.3a* and *Biology 2*, chapter 3). In other animal

species, the population initially grows at a rate of increase related to the reproductive rate of the species. Plotting the log of the numbers of individuals in the population against a linear plot of time gives a straight line (*figure 1.3b*). Eventually there will be **competition** for resources that are in limited supply. This competition is **intraspecific** because it occurs between individuals belonging to the one species. The result of this increasing competition is that the population growth slows down. Eventually the population should reach the maximum size that the environment can sustain, a figure known as the environment's **carrying capacity**. The population may overshoot the numbers the environment can support, but will then fall to stabilise at the carrying capacity.

However, human population biology is more complex, and seems to have gone through differ-ent phases of growth. As you can see from *figure 1.4*, anthropologists and archaeologists think that the world's human population was stable, or only rising very slowly, up to about 10 000 years ago and that it was rather small – somewhere between 5 and 10 million. Archaeological evidence indicates that about 10 000 years ago the popula-tion started to rise more rapidly; there was a change in the rate of increase of population and in the carrying capacity. This reflects the change

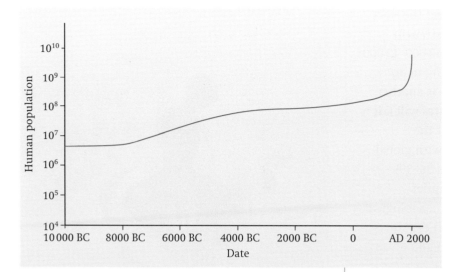

● **Figure 1.4** The world human population over time on a log-normal plot.

from mobile gatherer-hunter societies towards a more stationary agricultural lifestyle and the gradual development of the first towns and cities. There was another change in about 1750 with the onset of the industrial revolution. Since then world population has continued to rise sharply.

On 12th October 1999, the world population officially reached 6 billion. That's six thousand million of us. Every day, the number increases by about 250 000. In other words, each day a quarter of a million more people are born than die. We in the West are used to thinking that this is a problem of developing countries. It is true that most industrialised countries, such as the UK, the USA and France, have population growth rates that are low compared to those in other countries. Bangladesh's population, for example, is growing 12 times faster than that of the UK. Yet the average person in the industrialised world uses about 60 times more resources than someone in the developing world.

What is the carrying capacity of the UK for people? The current population of the UK is 59 million, but we have to import a large proportion of our food. Under intensive cultivation, agricultural self-sufficiency could support around 41 million people (see pages 13–15). In other words, given a population of 41 million we should be able to provide all our nutritional needs, provided we carried on farming intensively using fertilisers and pesticides (see page 28). A less

intensive use of our land, which might prevent the net loss of soil through soil erosion, would probably mean a population of, at most, 35 million.

So the carrying capacity of the UK estimated from food supply may be somewhere between 35 and 41 million people. However, if we had to rely on renewable energy sources (wind, solar, tidal, wave and geothermal) rather than on fossil fuels (coal, gas, oil and peat) or nuclear power we would probably have to reduce our population to 15–20 million.

Such a reduction may seem far-fetched, though it is interesting to note that only immigration is preventing the populations of many industrialised Western European countries from falling. It has been argued that the quality of life would be much better in the UK if there were only half or a third the number of people there are today. Imagine if this were the case. There would be less pollution, more room for wildlife and no more getting stuck in traffic jams.

SAQ 1.3

If the world's population is increasing in size by about 250 000 a day, how many is that in a year?

The effects of human activity

Agriculture

Britain during the last Ice Age was treeless. Scotland and northern England were covered in a great ice sheet and the south of England was a cold, windswept landscape. After the climate warmed and the ice melted, trees colonised the area from southern and eastern Europe and dense woodland developed. At lower latitudes, in the tropics, the climate became warmer and wetter and tropical forests flourished.

The 'magic' date of 10 000 years ago, when plants and animals started to be domesticated and the human population began to rise significantly (*figure*

1.4), marks the end of the last Ice Age and the start of the warm period we live in today. Past warm periods, the interglacials, lasted about 12 000–15 000 years. We do not yet know if we are living in an interglacial, as we do not know if there is another glacial coming, when global temperatures will fall and the ice caps expand over Britain. At the moment humans are more concerned with global warming than global cooling (see pages 36–39).

In the Near East 10 000 years ago a quiet revolution was about to take place. Archaeological excavations have revealed villages with evidence of early cereal crops and herded sheep and goats: farming had begun. As farming spread, human lifestyles changed and population densities increased (see pages 3–5). Gradually the natural vegetation of many areas was modified and replaced due to the action of farmers grazing their animals and planting crops (see pages 9–11).

Agriculture seems to have first made an impact in Britain between 6000 and 5000 years ago. The gradual replacement of natural vegetation as a result of cultivation occurred throughout the next 3000 years with the introduction of ploughs, then better ploughs, and the increasing use of animals for ploughing and transport, milk and wool. By the time William I had the census taken which is recorded in the Domesday Book of 1086, only about 15% of England retained its original woodland. Intensive farming is now the normal method of food production in most of Europe and North America. Some of the biosocial consequences of modern agricultural practices are discussed in chapter 2.

Not every culture farms intensively. There are some groups, including the many small tribes of the Amazon basin and the Inuit of the Arctic, who still live in ways similar to those of our ancestral gatherer-hunters. Some, like the Dinka and Maasai in Africa, and nomads in the Middle East and Mongolia, herd animals, be they cattle, goats, camels or horses (*figure 1.5*). Many groups in South America, India, Africa and elsewhere grow mixtures of crops local to their area such as maize, cassava, sorghum, rice, vegetables and fruits, to meet their immediate needs.

Whatever way of life a group has, whether gatherer-hunter or of industrial complexity, it is

● **Figure 1.5** Cattle are central to the lives of the Dinka people in the Sudan, Africa.

important that their way of life is **sustainable**. Hunters must never overhunt their prey, gatherers must leave enough seed for the next harvest, herds must not damage their grazing land beyond recovery, villagers must not take all the trees for firewood, intensive farming must not lead to soil erosion and dustbowl creation, and industry must not pollute the land, rivers or seas beyond repair. You can judge for yourself just how sustainable many human activities are as you read the rest of this book.

Pollution

Almost any substance can become a **pollutant** if it occurs in the wrong place, in the wrong concentration or at the wrong time. Hence fertilisers are excellent substances for increasing crop yields in intensive agricultural systems, but the same fertilisers running off the land into a river can pollute the water and cause the death of organisms in the natural ecosystem. Farming pollutants include fertilisers, pesticides and animal waste. Our domestic lifestyle produces distinctive pollutants too – domestic refuse, car exhaust fumes and chlorofluorocarbons (CFCs) from refrigerators and aerosol sprays.

Pollution from industrial processes has been around longer than you might think. Metal extraction was known as early as 6000 years ago and metal pollution has been found deep in the ice of Greenland, which is about 4000 years old! The Romans were determined polluters. They burned coal in their underfloor heating systems and smelted all sorts of heavy metal ores to extract lead, copper, silver and zinc. Smelting ores in open fires and crude furnaces was an inefficient process that produced considerable atmospheric pollution. Although huge quantities of metals are now smelted compared with Roman times, luckily for us the methods of extraction have improved. Metal extraction is more efficient, so more metal is extracted even from poorer grade ores and less contaminating metal escapes during the process. Pollution is, however, still a big problem in the world as you can see in chapter 3.

Threats to biodiversity

Biodiversity is a much-heard word these days, although it was probably first used as recently as 1985. It is really shorthand for biological diversity. Biological diversity can be measured at all sorts of levels: the diversity of ecosystems in a region, the number of species in each ecosystem, and the genetic diversity within the populations of each species. Biodiversity includes all these levels of complexity and can be assessed on a local, national or global scale.

Ecologists and conservationists are very concerned about the threatened and actual loss of global biodiversity. The activities of humans over the last 100 000 years have severely compromised biodiversity. Hunting large animals for food probably led to the extinction of species such as mammoths and giant, flightless birds. Clearing

● **Figure 1.6** Coral reefs like this one off Cozumel Island, Mexico, have a high biodiversity of animals and algae. Reefs are under threat from excess sediments and pollution carried out to sea by large rivers.

natural vegetation for farmland and dwelling space and the polluting of soil, sea and atmosphere have all had the effect of reducing biodiversity (*figure 1.6*). We still have no certain idea how many species there are in the world or what many of those species are. Estimates vary a lot, but there may be as many as 15 million species, of which eight million are insects.

By far the most diverse places on land (we are not so sure about the sea as the very deep oceans are mostly unexplored) are the tropical rainforests and the largest, in the Amazon basin of South America, is the richest of all. We have still not studied the rainforests enough to know exactly what is there, or how their ecosystems function. Yet it is these forests that are disappearing at an alarming rate, cleared for subsistence farming, for cattle ranching, for timber extraction, for mining, for access, and by accidental burning.

The issues involved in conserving ecosystems and the biodiversity of UK habitats are discussed in chapter 5. Chapter 6 discusses the global aspects.

SAQ 1.4
State the three levels and the three scales at which biodiversity can be measured.

Monitoring the environment

Ecology is in many ways the most complicated of all the biological sciences. Ecologists have to know something about the structure, physiology and behaviour of organisms before they can begin to understand how such organisms interact with one another and with the physical environment. For these reasons, ecology is increasingly an *experimental* science. Ecologists constantly need to test their predictions either in natural environments, in semi-natural experiments out in the field, or in artificial, simplified laboratory experiments.

Theories can be of great value in ecology, but they must always be tested against reality, and this is where practical ecology is so important. We can only gain an understanding about the ecosystems around us by getting information about them through practical ecology. However, whole eco-systems are often far too complex to understand all in one go. It is easier to begin by choosing one or two species, or a small area of habitat, to study in detail. Practical ecology involves making obser-vations, taking measurements and sometimes testing ideas by experimentation.

Because there is so much to study in the environment and because the environment may change considerably in the next few decades (due to global warming and pollution) anyone can do valuable research. Carefully designed and long-term observations can be of great value. Just recording when the first bluebells start to flower and the first tree leaves appear, how often late frosts damage leaves or when frogs spawn each year could be important records of the effects of changing climate. As Oliver Rackham, a leading expert on ancient woodland, put it: 'I often lament the observations which I would have begun if I had known in the 1960s what were to be the ecological problems of the 1990s ... I would urge conservation trusts to be more active in long-term research, experimentation and maintaining archives ... pho-tographing from fixed points, recording perma-nently marked plots or transects, or following the fate of marked individual plants.' (*Nature in Cambridgeshire*, 1999, volume 41, page 86.)

Chapter 7 shows how investigative ecology can be pursued.

SUMMARY

◆ Ecology is the study of organisms in their natural surroundings.

◆ Environmental biology includes the study of humans in the environment.

◆ The number of people in the world now exceeds six billion and is still increasing rapidly.

◆ The carrying capacity of the UK for people is difficult to determine and depends on whether one means the carrying capacity with respect to sustainable food production or renewable energy resources.

◆ Agriculture first made an impact in Britain between 6000 and 5000 years ago.

◆ Humans have had a significant effect on biodiversity for tens of thousands of years.

◆ Environmental monitoring, especially if carried out over many years, can make a major contribution to ecology and conservation.

Questions

1 a Distinguish between the terms habitat and niche.
   b How might you investigate the niche of a particular species of garden slug?

2 Describe how the world's population of humans has changed over time and compare this with the equivalent data typical of other animal species.

CHAPTER 2

Agriculture and the environment

By the end of this chapter you should be able to:

1 explain the effects of burning, mowing and grazing in the maintenance of a deflected succession;

2 distinguish between extensive and intensive food production;

3 assess the practice of intercropping, and the use of legumes in crop rotation, as methods of cultivating crops;

4 appreciate the implications of intensive food production in terms of the effects of farm waste on the environment, land reclamation and the destruction of hedgerows;

5 assess the advantages and disadvantages of organic farming;

6 explain the principles, and assess the advantages and disadvantages, of biological pest control.

The effects of farming on the environment

The development of farming

Until 5000 to 10000 years ago, humans obtained their food by gathering plant material and hunting for animals – they were gatherer-hunters. In Britain they ate a mixed diet of nuts, berries, fish and shellfish and occasionally killed wild cattle and deer. We think that to attract deer, the hunters cut down groups of trees and returned weeks later when the stumps had sprouted new shoots on which the deer could feast. This was the start of forest clearance.

After agriculture spread into Britain between 5000 and 6000 years ago, deforestation in the lowlands for crop growing began, first on the easily ploughed sandy soils and finally on the heavy clays. All that is left of the once extensive forests are a few scattered woods (*figure 1.1* on page 1), either surrounded by farmland or on steep valley sides too difficult to farm. Global deforestation still continues nowadays, with the destruction of tropical rainforest and other forest types.

In the early stages of animal domestication, humans must have semi-tamed wild animals, perhaps by taking and hand-rearing their young. Dogs joined us early – maybe 14000 years ago – followed about 9000 to 10000 years ago by cattle, sheep and goats. Once animals were herded together, farmers selected, either consciously or without realising it, for various traits, including lack of aggression, high milk yields, softer wool, and so on. Eventually selective breeding accelerated these changes as farmers realised they could breed from their best stock. The same was true of crops – a progression from gathering seed from the wild, to selecting and storing home-grown seed, to cross-pollinating plants deliberately. Now we have all the tools of scientific research to aid these processes: tissue culture, artificial insemination, genetic engineering, and so on.

The production of **inorganic chemical fertilisers** revolutionised farming methods. The first enriched fertilisers were made in the 1840s by dissolving bones and phosphate-rich rocks in sulphuric acid to produce superphosphates, but the main development of chemical fertilisers came during the Second World War. Fertilisers provide additional nitrogen, phosphorus and potassium for the soil. Such nutrients are almost always in short supply so any addition improves plant growth and yields.

Good farming practice and consumer demand increasingly requires uniformity of crops for ease of harvesting, high yield, synchronous ripening and long storage life. This has led to the development of monocultures – large fields of a single, genetically uniform crop, heavily fertilised and sprayed with pesticides (*figure 2.1*). In livestock rearing, maximum growth rates, increased muscle mass and high milk yields are required.

Deflected successions

Succession is the natural change in the structure and species composition of a community over time (*Biology 2*, chapter 4). This definition excludes changes that are the immediate, direct result of human activity. For instance, changes such as ploughing, tree felling and crop planting are all excluded.

● **Figure 2.1** East Anglia has some of the most intensively farmed land in the UK.

Succession that starts on bare, uncolonised ground or in newly formed lakes, both of which lack soil or vegetation, is known as **primary succession**. Examples of primary succession today can be found in the establishment of organisms in such habitats as sand dunes, volcanic lava flows, landslides and bare areas left by retreating glaciers and ice sheets. Succession in an area where the vegetation has been destroyed, but where soil, seeds and burrowing animals may survive, is called **secondary succession**. Such succession might occur after fire or flooding or in areas covered by volcanic ash.

Left to develop naturally, both primary and secondary succession will usually continue until a mature and stable vegetation type develops. Such a community will be typical for the particular climatic conditions in the area and is sometimes called the **climatic climax community**. Succession does not always result in the establishment of a climax community. Much grassland, for example, is maintained by human activities like **burning**, **mowing** or **controlled grazing** (*figure 2.2*). With the removal of these activities, grassland is usually colonised by scrub and develops into forest. Burning, mowing and grazing keep the grass short and prevent tree seedlings from establishing. For this reason, grassland is said to be the result of **deflected succession** and is described as a **plagioclimax**.

Grassland can be maintained by many grazing species: sheep, goats, cattle, horses and llamas. Each species has its own distinctive grazing behaviour. Sheep prefer short grass, which they cut with their front teeth, and tend to select the most nourishing flowering shoots. Cows prefer longer grass, which they can rip out using their tongues, but they can nibble shorter grass if necessary.

Nutrient-poor grassland can be very rich in plant species (*figure 5.3* on page 56). The constant nibbling encourages finer grasses, while broad-leaved flowering plants are more likely to thrive if grazing occurs in autumn and winter rather than in spring and summer when they are producing flowers and seeds. One effect of feeding cattle with additional food concentrates to maintain high animal densities on the land is that the enriched cowpats increase the nutrient content of

● **Figure 2.2** The picturesque scenery of Swaledale in the Yorkshire Dales National Park is made up of deflected successions. In the foreground is a hay meadow, behind it are fields grazed by sheep and cattle. The upland moors in the background are grazed by sheep and managed for grouse shooting.

the soil. This can lead to the development of nutrient-rich but species-poor grassland.

Overstocking means putting more animals on the grazing land than the growth rate of the grasses can support. This leads to damage of the vegetation – bare areas appear where grasses have been over-eaten or scraped up by many hooves. The soil is then susceptible to erosion by wind and rain. Grazing animals, especially goats, can cause considerable damage to vegetation. This is particularly true on small remote islands where introduced goats can eat the rare native floras to extinction. Saint Helena in the South Atlantic is one such example. Goats were introduced in the sixteenth century by sailors and have since then severely damaged the native vegetation, which was rich in endemic species found only on that island.

In Australia, today's vegetation is thought to be largely the result of thousands of years of controlled burning by Aboriginals. The last 200 years have seen much damage done to these fragile dry ecosystems by more harmful and too frequent burning by European settlers, plus overgrazing by millions of sheep and cattle and by plagues of introduced rabbits. In the late 1990s, Australian farmers released a virus (a calcivirus), which they hope will kill all the rabbits, just as their predecessors hoped myxomatosis would in the 1950s.

Much of upland Britain today is treeless, covered in heather, bracken, grasses and peat bog. These areas were colonised by birch, oak and hazel soon after the last Ice Age and their ancient tree stumps can still be found under the peat. It is thought the heather moors began to spread about 7000 years ago, when humans felled or burned the trees, and that this coincided with a wetter phase in the climate. Whatever triggered the change, what grew was a blanket of peat: *Sphagnum* moss, cottongrass and rushes in wetter areas; heather and grasses in drier parts.

Now these moors are largely used for recreation and sport (*figure 2.2*). Red grouse and deer are managed so they can be shot. The grouse live best in a patchwork of old heather for shelter and nesting, and new heather providing young shoots for food. The moors are maintained as a deflected succession by burning different areas each year to encourage the growth of new heather shoots, and this produces a mosaic of mature and developing vegetation. Because people pay for the privilege, grouse and deer shooting can be much more profitable than sheep farming, which is the alternative use of the moors. *Table 2.1* shows the animal density and production of Scottish heather moorland. The sheep and deer too, of course, help maintain the deflected succession.

Another example of a deflected succession leading to a plagioclimax is a hedge. Hedges are maintained by regular cutting back. A hedge that is left for more than a few years develops into a line of trees. This may have consequences for smaller

Animal	Density in spring (per km²)	Number of young (per km²)	Yield for food (kg per km²)
Sheep	50	40	1000
Red deer	10	2	110
Red grouse	65	89	25

● **Table 2.1** Spring densities, the density of young and the yield for food of three commercial species of animals on heather moorland in the highlands of Scotland.

plants and other organisms found there, as a line of trees provides a different set of habitats from a hedge (see pages 17–18).

SAQ 2.1

Suggest what effect the following might have on the numbers of grouse, and why: **a** more frequent burning; **b** less frequent burning of moors.

Food production

Methods of food production

In the world today you can find the whole spectrum of ways of obtaining food in different human societies.

In the Arctic the last of the great hunters, the Inuit, have a diet that is almost exclusively meat, with just a few summer berries. They catch seals and fish through holes in the sea ice and hunt caribou. Their clothing, too, is provided by the animals they catch. Very few Inuit now live by traditional ways – many are involved in the oil-fields of Alaska and most have moved into small towns, rather than living in snow igloos, and use modern technology such as rifles and snowmobiles.

At the other extreme of climate, in the hot, wet tropical forests of the Amazon, small tribes live as true gatherer-hunters on nuts and fruits, monkey meat and other food they gather from the forest. They live in a sustainable way, although their lifestyle does not support very high population numbers. These tribes do not cope well with the cultures and diseases of foreigners: a shocking estimate is that one tribe a year has been lost since 1900. The rubber-tappers of Brazil also use the forest as gatherers but in a commercial way. They collect rubber, Brazil nuts and palm hearts and hunt fish. They work the forest in a systematic way and most have leases from the Brazilian government that bind them to protecting the forest and ban them from clear-felling the trees for timber. The forest used sustainably like this is a renewable resource and makes more money per hectare than clear-felling for timber or ranching (see pages 72–74).

In some tropical forests subsistence farmers eke out a living in small-scale slash and burn clearings where they plant crops in the ashes (*figure 2.3*). This too is sustainable if the cleared areas are not too large and are left to regenerate for many years after use. Clearings usually have to be abandoned after three to five years as the forest soil is nutrient-poor and soon becomes infertile. Such shifting cultivation is common in Latin America, Africa and parts of Asia but is under pressure as population densities increase (see pages 4–5). Instead of allowing clearings to regenerate and recover their fertility, which takes about 20 years, areas are being re-cleared more frequently – sometimes after only five years of rest. The fertility of these overused sites is improved by adding animal manure or leafy tree branches; most subsistence farmers cannot afford chemical fertilisers.

In many areas, herding is a way of life. In the Andes, alpacas provide beautiful, soft and highly valued wool, while llamas are used more as pack animals for transporting the crops of potatoes (our familiar larger potatoes were developed from these Andean tubers) down the mountains for

● **Figure 2.3** A clearing in the Amazon forest is being created by cutting and burning the natural vegetation. It will be cultivated for 3–5 years before soil fertility is exhausted when the farmer will abandon the clearing and create another.

trade. In central Africa, herds of cattle represent great wealth on the hoof and are a key part of the social life of peoples such as the Maasai and Dinka (*figure 1.5* on page 6).

Throughout agricultural history, farmers have run small mixed farms that produce a range of foodstuffs intended to support a family through-out the year and provide extra for barter or sale. Generations of practice have resulted in many clever farming skills for maximising yields and minimising pest problems, including the use of intercropping (see below).

Usually these farming methods have been sustainable, allowing farms to continue for gener-ations, although there have been some notable examples of farming disasters in the past. About 4000 years ago, in the Middle East, the Mesopotamians managed to destroy their soil fertility by over-irrigating it until it turned salty (salination). In Central America, the Mayans grew maize too intensively until the soil just washed away (erosion) and their civilisation collapsed in about AD 850. Something similar happened to create the dust bowl in the Midwest of the US in the 1930s.

Intercropping

Many small farms increase their yields by growing more than one crop in the same field at the same time, a process known as **intercropping**. The different crops are either grown all mixed together, or in more orderly rows. This is an ancient method of cultivation that has probably continued unchanged for centuries in many parts of the world (*figure 2.4*). It is especially common in tropical areas where the growing season lasts all year round.

The principle of intercropping is to increase the overall yield of the land available by growing different and complementary plants together: short and tall, annuals and perennials, legumes and high nitrogen-requirers. Usually between two and six different crop plants are grown. In central Africa these include millet, sorghum, peanuts, sweet potato, cowpeas, soya beans and cotton. Often one crop plant is ready to eat before another ripens, so tall crops like maize or cassava can be harvested and the plants removed before the shorter crops like sweet potatoes and beans begin to ripen. The mixes usually include legumes (peas and beans) that have root nodules, which probably increase the yields of other crops by supplying them with fixed nitrogen (see pages 20–21 and *Biology 1* pages 97–98). One plant species may protect another from strong sunlight, heavy rain and wind, provide a habitat for predators of pests, be a support for climbing crops or attract pollinators. Because the crops are harvested at different times, the soil is protected from erosion, as it is never bare. This also means that weeds are kept under control.

In parts of the United States, intercropping is used as a way of lessening the effects of pests that normally build up in vast areas of monocultures. Large fields are divided into strips planted alter-nately with crops such as maize and peanuts. Intercropping like this can reduce pest damage by up to 80%, possibly because the predators for pests of one crop hide in the other.

SAQ 2.2

Would you expect intercropping to work best when crops with similar or different niches are grown? Explain your answer.

Extensive and intensive farming

Farming systems vary tremendously in the amount of fertilisers and pesticides that are applied and in the yields obtained. *Table 2.2* shows how different the average amounts of fertiliser application can be in different countries. **Extensive farming** is the production of crops and

● **Figure 2.4** A mixture of crops, including date palms, growing in the El Humra Oasis, Sudan.

	1980	1984	1990	1994
Australia	27	26	26	35
China	144	200	284	309
Ecuador	30	29	28	51
Egypt	268	341	361	264
Ethiopia	3	2	7	14
India	33	49	73	80
Ireland	536	649	725	569
Japan	412	440	402	398
Korea, North	397	398	409	377
Korea, South	368	361	440	472
Madagascar	3	2	3	4
Nepal	10	18	27	33
Netherlands	828	851	614	592
Nigeria	5	9	12	9
Pakistan	52	62	89	98
Uganda	0	0	0	0
UK	316	371	350	381
USA	108	104	99	103
Zimbabwe	59	52	56	59

● **Table 2.2** Annual fertiliser application (kg) per hectare of land under cultivation, for selected countries.

livestock raised on land which has little or no fertiliser added. The farmer relies on the natural fertility of the soils and on recycling nutrients within the system. Usually the annual yields from extensive farming are very low (measured at about 1–20 kg of nitrogen per hectare: the amount of nitrogen in the crop is sometimes used as a measure of output as nitrogen is such an important element in nutrient cycling, as shown in *Biology 1*, chapter 7). Extensive farming includes upland sheep, Andean llamas and alpacas, grain production in semi-arid areas, conifer forestry, deciduous woodland and some low-productivity dairy and meat farms.

Extensive sheep farming is now common in all upland areas of

the UK. It involves large areas of land that are not fertilised. The cost of maintaining the land is low. However, as the grazing is of low quality, the stocking levels have to be low and productivity is also low. In fact, many upland areas are at risk from overstocking.

Farming, especially in heavily industrialised and populated areas such as North America, Japan and Europe, has changed considerably in the last few hundred years. There has been a trend away from subsistence farming towards larger farm units run by small numbers of people, but supplying food to the ever-growing towns and cities. The industrial revolution also caused a farming revolution as it supplied farmers with the chemicals and large machines they needed to farm intensively. Ever-increasing applications of fertilisers led to ever-increasing yields (*figure 2.5*), providing the food needed to feed the industrial factory and shop workers. This has resulted in a continuing increase in **intensive farming**. Intensive farming systems are open systems, because the large yields are exported from the farm, and there is a net loss of nutrients, which has to be replaced each year with fertilisers. In general, any system that uses more than 20 kg of fertiliser per hectare per year is classified as intensive. You can see from *table 2.2* which countries have little intensive farming.

Changing farm practices, together with the use of fertilisers, pesticide application and the

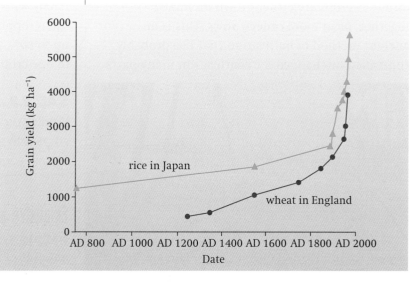

● **Figure 2.5** The increase in yields for rice in Japan and wheat in England over the last 1200 years. Note that yields only rose sharply after chemical fertiliser application became commonplace in the twentieth century.

introduction of new crop varieties, have been responsible for great increases in farm yields over the past 400 years and especially during the last 50 (*figure 2.5*). Yields from intensive farming vary tremendously from as little as 15–40 kg of nitrogen per hectare for lowland sheep, cattle and some dairy production, to over 150 kg of nitrogen per hectare for Japanese vegetable crops. In general, vegetable and grain farming – where the crops are photosynthetic producers – have higher yields than meat and dairy farming, where the producers are primary consumers one step further along the food chain (see chapter 1).

The steady increase in world grain production since 1950 began to falter in the 1990s. Indeed, during the 1990s grain yields fell slightly. This was due, in part, to a reduction in fertiliser use in some areas (*table 2.2*) and the break-up of the Soviet Union. Other reasons include the degradation of land due to soil erosion and an increase in summer heat waves, due possibly to the enhanced greenhouse effect (see pages 36–38). Lack of water for irrigation is already an important factor limiting farm production in some countries. The increasing loss of farming land for housing, leisure (e.g. golf courses) and industry may cause a decline in the amount of land available for farming; an amount that has remained remarkably consistent for decades.

The lowlands of Britain, most notably the flat, open expanses of East Anglia, are highly cultivated areas of intensive farming (*figure 2.1* on page 10). Such arable farms grow monocultures of highly specialised crop types, which are specially produced by suppliers to be genetically identical so that growth and ripening are uniform. The large fields were created by the removal of hedgerows (see page 17). To maximise yields, fields have applications of large doses of fertilisers and pesticides (see pages 28–29). Crops are harvested using large, heavy machinery (*figure 2.1*), which can compact and damage the soil.

For livestock farming the choice of breed is important – dairy cows are usually chosen to maximise milk yields, although some herds are bred for the cream content of their milk (Jersey and Guernsey cows, for example). There is much debate at the moment about the injection of cows with genetically engineered BST (a bovine growth hormone) that further increases milk production. This is now common practice in the US and some other countries, but has so far been banned in the European Union (EU).

Breeds of sheep, cattle, pigs and poultry have been selected which have terrific rates of growth and bulky muscles. Many such animals are never intended to survive to maturity and there is concern for their welfare as their bones are sometimes not strong enough to hold their weight. Similar concern is expressed for egg-laying battery hens, kept at high densities in cages and de-beaked to prevent them pecking each other to death.

Most intensively farmed animals are kept at much higher densities than is generally considered natural and the chances of them catching diseases due to stress and overcrowding are high. To counteract this, animals are often routinely fed with antibiotics, a practice which is now considered undesirable as it increases the selection of bacteria that are resistant to many antibiotics. This may make the treatment of human infections more difficult too.

SAQ 2.3

From *table 2.2*, determine: **a** which country has increased its fertiliser application the most (in units of $kg\,ha^{-1}\,yr^{-1}$); **b** which country has decreased its fertiliser application the most. Suggest why these trends have occurred.

The debate about the advantages and disadvantages of intensive versus extensive farming deepened in the late 1990s as the first genetically modified crops (**GM crops**) began to be grown commercially in the US, China and South America. By then, several large multinational companies, including Monsanto, had developed varieties of GM crops that were resistant to powerful herbicides such as **glyphosate**. The idea was that the herbicide could be sprayed on such crops, killing the weeds but not damaging the crop. The companies concerned have argued that this is advantageous for farmers *and* environmentally friendly, as herbicides such as glyphosate are less toxic to animals than alternative herbicides.

Many crops are also being genetically engineered to be resistant to pests and diseases.

For example, the European corn borer is an insect that is a major pest of maize, causing global losses of around $1 billion a year. Maize has been genetically engineered to be resistant to the European corn borer and is now being grown commercially in the US. The crop does not need to be sprayed with insecticides as often as conventional crops do – which should be good for the environment – and it seems to produce higher yields than its conventional, non-genetically engineered counterpart.

However, such arguments in favour of GM crops have not convinced the general public in Europe and trials designed to investigate the environmental consequences of GM crops have been intentionally damaged (*figure 2.6*). Environmental campaigning groups such as Greenpeace and Friends of the Earth have argued that crops genetically modified to be resistant to certain herbicides make farmers dependent on herbicides at a time when we should be decreasing, not increasing, our reliance on herbicides. In addition, fears have been expressed about the possibility of pollen from genetically modified crops contaminating organic crops (see page 18) and of modified crops interbreeding with native plants to form 'superweeds'.

Environmental implications of intensive farming

Farm waste

One of the problems of intensive food production is the increased risk of pollution to the environment from farm waste products. In arable farming, nitrogen fertilisers applied in large amounts to crops can build up in the soil. They end up being converted to nitrates by soil bacteria. The nitrates can then be transported via rainwater falling on the open soil of farmland into the stream and river systems.

Problem waste products from livestock farming include stackable manure (faeces and bedding) and slurry (a liquid mix of excreta, yard washings and rainwater). We have already mentioned how livestock can increase the fertility of grassland if fed concentrated feedstuffs (see page 10). When animals such as pigs, cattle or battery hens are kept in enclosed sheds or yards, the problem of manure disposal increases. Slurry is often collected and stored in large tanks or specially constructed 'ponds' called lagoons. In an ideal world all the slurry would be spread onto fields as fertiliser, but such manures often have the wrong ratio of N:P:K, usually too little nitrogen, too much phosphorus and potassium. In addition, specialisation in farming means that livestock farms with excess slurry are seldom near the arable farm with the need for fertiliser.

Inevitably there are accidental leakages, or even deliberate releases of excess waste, which get into nearby watercourses and cause eutrophication (see page 25 and *Biology 2*, chapter 3). Farm effluent is not only high in nitrates, but may contain traces of growth hormones and antibiotics. Both of these may have long-term consequences if persistently released into the environment, even in very small quantities. A novel idea is to catch the gases such as methane (biogases) emitted from the slurry and use them as fuel.

Land reclamation

In intensive farming regimes, fertile land is highly valued, so there is a strong drive to bring more land under intensive farming. Land normally under extensive farming can be 'improved' by ploughing and

● **Figure 2.6** Some environmental pressure groups have damaged trials designed to investigate the environmental consequences of GM crops.

fertilising. This can be a threat to traditional areas of beauty and is a problem in some National Parks (see page 57). More spectacular is the reclamation of low-lying wetlands. Very large areas of the Netherlands (the Polders) and the marshy fens around the Wash in the UK have been reclaimed by building retaining walls and pumping out the water. Reclamation started in Roman times, but the major drainage work occurred in the seventeenth century, when 2500 km² of fen was drained in the UK alone. Not only does this process destroy important marine and freshwater marsh habitats, but it also requires constant maintenance of the sea defences to prevent the sea retaking the land. If global warming causes an increase in sea levels due to melting of the polar ice caps (see page 38), then maintenance of these reclaimed areas could prove very costly indeed.

Another form of land reclamation is the improvement of degraded and polluted sites such as coal tips. This is discussed on pages 45–48.

Hedgerow destruction

A **hedgerow** is a narrow belt of vegetation dominated by a variety of shrubs, sometimes with occasional trees (*figure 2.7*). Hedgerows are the result of human activity and their history is a fascinating and complex subject. Traditionally they served two functions: as a barrier to the movement of livestock, and as a means of marking out the boundaries of property. Studies of ancient hedgerows have shown that there is a fairly constant rate of invasion of new species. So, to date a hedge, measure out a 30 m length, count the number of woody species in that length and multiply by 100 to get the age of the hedge in years. Of course a newly created hedge wonderfully designed by an ecologist with lots of species would give you a spurious age!

Because so much of Britain is dominated by fields, hedgerows in the lowlands and dry stone walls in upland areas (*figure 2.2* on page 11) are of great ecological significance. They are a home for large numbers of species and often act as essential **wildlife corridors** connecting scattered woods and copses. Amongst the plants in British hedges are shrubs such as blackthorn, hawthorn and hazel, and smaller plants such as primrose, lords

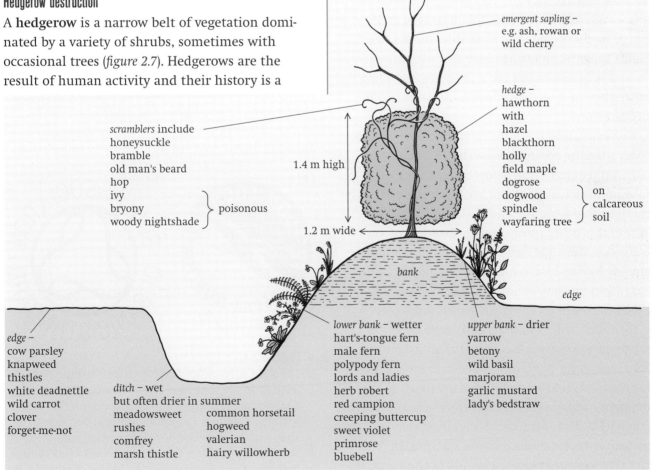

scramblers include
honeysuckle
bramble
old man's beard
hop
ivy
bryony } poisonous
woody nightshade }

1.4 m high

1.2 m wide

emergent sapling –
e.g. ash, rowan or
wild cherry

hedge –
hawthorn
with
hazel
blackthorn
holly
field maple
dogrose
dogwood } on
spindle } calcareous
wayfaring tree } soil

bank

edge

edge –
cow parsley
knapweed
thistles
white deadnettle
wild carrot
clover
forget-me-not

ditch – wet
but often drier in summer
meadowsweet
rushes
comfrey
marsh thistle

common horsetail
hogweed
valerian
hairy willowherb

lower bank – wetter
hart's-tongue fern
male fern
polypody fern
lords and ladies
herb robert
red campion
creeping buttercup
sweet violet
primrose
bluebell

upper bank – drier
yarrow
betony
wild basil
marjoram
garlic mustard
lady's bedstraw

● **Figure 2.7** Diagram showing the plants found in a typical old hedge and ditch in the south of England.

Bird species	Mammal species
hedge sparrow	wood mouse
house sparrow	field vole
wren	common vole
robin	bank vole
blackbird	common shrew
song thrush	pygmy shrew
blue tit	brown rat
great tit	hedgehog
long-tailed tit	mole
chaffinch	rabbit
bullfinch	stoat
greenfinch	weasel
goldfinch	fox
linnet	badger
yellowhammer	
wood pigeon	

● **Table 2.3** Animals which breed in hedgerows in Britain.

and ladies, hart's-tongue fern and garlic mustard (*figure 2.7*). Vertebrates that live in hedges and hedge banks include the bank vole, shrews, wren, hedge sparrow, yellowhammer and whitethroat (*table 2.3*). Invertebrates are numerous, including butterflies such as the brimstone, orange tip and hedge brown.

Unfortunately, the large farm machinery in use today (like the combine harvester in *figure 2.1* on page 10) requires large fields. Hedges are seen to take up valuable space and are often removed. It is thought that from the end of the Second World War to the 1980s approximately 8000 km of hedgerow were lost each year in the UK. Despite already having lost so many hedges, conservation organisations have estimated that in the 1990s losses were still totalling 5000–6000 km a year.

However, hedges have recently seen a resurgence. Research has shown that hedgerows are habitats for pollinators of certain crops and for predators and parasites of many pests, so that removing hedgerows may therefore actually *reduce* crop yields. Farmers have also realised that hedgerow removal can increase soil erosion. The fact that hedgerows have a beauty of their own is becoming more widely appreciated and as they

need not be restricted to farmland, their planting is being encouraged, especially in urban areas. Many new hedges are being planted and several metropolitan authorities have signed a Wildlife Trust Hedge Pledge supporting their hedgerows.

Organic farming

Brief history

There are really two categories of **organic farming**. The first has been practised since farming developed. Indeed, it was the natural form of farming all over the world, wherever people tilled the soil or tended animals. Many small-scale and subsistence farmers still farm organically, partly because they are continuing the traditional methods of their ancestors, and partly because they are too poor to buy chemical fertilisers and pesticides.

The second category is of recent development and has arisen in reaction to modern methods of intensive farming (see page 14). Many people feel that intensive farming is damaging the environment and want to move towards what they perceive as a less destructive and more healthy lifestyle. This includes choosing food that has been produced with animal welfare in mind (free-range eggs and chickens or RSPCA Freedom Food (*figure 2.8a*), for example) and organic produce.

The aims of this second category of organic farming are to produce food crops by building up

● **Figure 2.8**
a The RSPCA Freedom Food logo indicating products from animals that have lived with freedom from distress, pain, hunger and thirst, discomfort and with the freedom to express normal behaviour. They may or may not be raised organically.
b The Soil Association Organic Standard Mark, which indicates that the food on sale has been organically produced to strict European Union standards.

soil fertility using the minimum of non-renewable resources (which also means no synthetic chemicals) and with minimum damage to the environment (which includes minimal pollution). Farmers must also show respect for animal welfare and work *with* nature rather than against it. To be able to state that their food is organically produced requires the farmers to register with a monitoring association and fulfil several criteria governed by EU regulation, which are implemented by the UK Register of Organic Food Standards. In Britain, over 2000 farmers are registered with the Soil Association, which is the largest organic certification body (*figure 2.8b*) and provides advice and guidelines for farmers wishing to convert to organic production.

To qualify for the Register of Organic Food Standards, farmers must fulfil various requirements:

■ There must be a conversion time of two years before land previously farmed with synthetic chemicals can be called organic. This causes a problem as during this 'transition time' the land has to be farmed organically, so the yields tend to be lower, but the produce cannot yet be sold as organic. The Ministry of Agriculture, Fisheries and Food (MAFF) have an Organic Farming Scheme that can assist farmers with financial help during conversion.

■ The organic crops must be physically separated from non-organic crops to minimise cross-contamination.

■ Records must be kept and the land and records inspected by an approved body (like the Soil Association).

There are also strict requirements about processing and labelling food for sale. Food imported from other countries must also reach these standards. About 70% of organic foodstuffs sold in the UK are imported.

Organic farming requires an understanding of how soil fertility can be built up and maintained without the aid of synthetic fertilisers. Organic farmers use traditional methods, especially **crop rotation**, where a different crop is grown in a field each year. Once every few years a crop of legumes is used to increase the nitrogen content of the soil by perhaps 100–200 kg ha^{-1} in that year

(see pages 20–21) and animal manure fertiliser is applied. Crop rotation reduces the survival of weeds, pests and diseases specific to particular crops – a form of biological pest control (see page 21) used in organic farming. Non-synthetic substances such as sulphur can also be sprayed on crops for pest control.

Most organic farms have livestock, so their organic manure can be used. The nutrient value of grazing land is maintained using clover (another legume). Animal health and welfare are considered very important so, although natural remedies are preferred to treat sick animals, conventional medicines must be used if necessary. The routine application of antibiotics, vaccines and worming compounds is not allowed.

While the original organic farms were small-scale subsistence farms, often with intercropping, modern organic farming can look like intensive farming. Compared with intensive farms, stocking levels of animals are lower and yields are usually lower too, but European organic farms in fertile areas such as the Netherlands can include large fields of monocultures.

Advantages of organic farming

Organic farming offers advantages both to the environment and consumers.

Advantages to the environment

■ The absence of synthetic pesticides and the careful use of organic pesticides mean that wildlife is encouraged on organic farms.

■ There is probably less risk of overuse of organic fertilisers than of synthetic ones and consequently a reduced risk of polluting nearby water systems.

■ Low levels of pesticide application may mean that more soil organisms survive, producing a better soil structure and hence increased inherent soil fertility.

■ More above-ground insects survive, most of which are harmless to the crop but provide more food for spiders, birds and other predators.

Advantages to consumers

■ There are no residues of synthetic pesticides on the surfaces of vegetables (but organic foods are not tested as rigorously as non-organic foods, so may have residues of substances permitted on organic farms).

■ The use of fewer airborne chemical sprays may help asthma sufferers.

■ There is a 'feel-good factor' of helping to improve the environment.

But note – the flavour of organic produce is no better than non-organic, and organic food may be no more nutritious or less harmful than well-washed non-organic food.

Disadvantages of organic farming

Despite its green image, organic farming has certain disadvantages.

Disadvantages to the environment

■ Some approved pesticides (sulphur) are non-specific so will harm non-target wildlife if used.

■ Organic farming produces lower yields than intensive farming so more land needs to be cultivated to provide the same amount of food. Is it better to have more land under organic crops, or smaller areas of intensively farmed land with the 'spare' used as nature reserves, woods, ponds, set-aside, etc.? This question may be especially relevant in developing countries where natural ecosystems may still be abundant but under threat from extensive (i.e. low-yield) farming.

Disadvantages to consumers

■ Organic farmers may only be able to grow the most disease-resistant strains of crops, reducing customer choice and possibly restricting taste.

■ Organic farming is labour intensive (this may be advantageous to farm workers of course) and thus expensive to buy.

■ Organic vegetables may have more blemishes and a shorter shelf life as they carry more fungal rot organisms than a well-sprayed non-organic vegetable. Retailers may be reluctant to hold too much stock and will push prices up to cover losses from decay. Purchasers may have to be more organised and not buy in bulk other-wise they are likely to end up throwing some onto the compost heap.

■ Organic vegetables may carry more wildlife: not everyone likes to pick off the cabbage white

caterpillars before they boil their broccoli. (Even worse to find them after boiling!) Build-up of bacteria due to use of manure as fertilizer may also be a health hazard.

■ Current choice of organic produce in shops is relatively low due to the small share of the market taken by organic foods (but choice is improving in the range of vegetables and especially in packaged and bottled goods).

Legumes in crop rotation

Rhizobium is the most important genus of **nitrogen-fixing bacteria**, that is bacteria that fix gaseous nitrogen. As shown in *Biology 1*, chapter 7, **nitrogen fixation** by bacteria is the reduction of the nitrogen found in the atmosphere, N_2, to the ammonium ion, NH_4^+. Nitrogen-fixing bacteria are of great ecological significance as they are the only natural way in which nitrogen fixation occurs apart from lightning (which produces nitrogen oxides). Without these natural processes, organisms would be unable to access the huge reserves of atmospheric nitrogen. Life as we know it would simply not exist as plants would be unable to make the various molecules, such as proteins and nucleic acids, that require nitrogen.

The bacteria in the genus *Rhizobium* live in the **root nodules** of many leguminous plants (*figure 2.9*) including such important crop plants as peas, beans, clovers and peanuts (groundnuts). The relationship seems to be a mutualistic one,

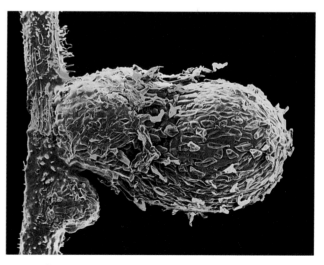

● **Figure 2.9** A scanning electron micrograph of a root nodule, caused by *Rhizobium*, on a pea plant (magnification ×12).

benefiting both the plants and the bacteria. The plants grow faster and can often colonise early successional habitats that are difficult for other flowering plants because of the nutrient-poor status of the soil. Plants that lack nitrogen-fixing bacteria, for example grasses, tend to arrive later in the succession.

The bacteria benefit by being provided with a protective home in the root nodules and ideal conditions for nitrogen fixation, as described below. In addition, the bacteria receive sugars from their hosts. Investigations have shown that *Rhizobium* can survive in soil in the absence of host plants where the bacteria feed **saprotrophically**, living off the remains of dead organisms. However, the proximity of a damaged leguminous root cell enables the bacteria to invade the legume. The plant then produces root nodules (*figure 2.9*). These root nodules are necessary for the bacteria to fix nitrogen. They contain **leghaemoglobin**, which functions rather like our own haemoglobin in that it traps oxygen. In the root nodules its role is to prevent too much oxygen from reaching the enzymes that fix the nitrogen. This is important because these enzymes are destroyed by oxygen, possibly because the nitrogen molecule (N_2) and the oxygen molecule (O_2) are similar in size and shape.

The enzyme responsible for nitrogen fixation is called **nitrogenase**. Plant breeders have dreamt for years of being able to breed the ability to fix nitrogen into the world's major non-leguminous crops, such as rice, wheat and maize. They hope to increase yields and reduce the financial and environmental costs of applying nitrogen-based fertilisers to the soil. With the advent of **genetic engineering** this dream has seemed more attainable. It has been suggested that the genes necessary for nitrogen fixation could be transferred from the bacteria to the crop plant, rather as the gene for insulin synthesis has been successfully transferred from humans to bacteria, allowing the manufacture by bacteria of human insulin for people with juvenile-onset diabetes.

Unfortunately there are no fewer than 17 genes responsible for the synthesis of nitrogenase! Although its chemical structure is still not completely known, nitrogenase is clearly a most

complex protein. This is probably because it is very difficult to break open the nitrogen molecule, which is extremely stable. It is thought that as many as 16 molecules of ATP are required to fix one molecule of N_2.

Biological pest control

What is biological control?

Modern intensive farming methods require chemical controls to keep pests at low levels so that crops are saleable. Unfortunately all these chemical applications not only kill pests, they also kill harmless organisms and even beneficial predators. Such predators would naturally keep down the numbers of pests by **biological control**, reducing the need for so many pesticides. This is one of the methods that organic farmers use to keep pests under control. Pests that can be so controlled include insects, fungi, nematodes and weeds. In open farmland, basic biological control simply entails encouraging the natural wildlife predators to visit and increase in number to levels that will keep the pests in check. For example, hoverfly larvae and ladybirds, both larvae and adults, eat greenfly, and starlings will pick leatherjacket grubs out of lawns. All these predators can be encouraged into a garden or, on a larger scale, into open fields, by providing extra food or hibernating spaces. Other organisms that control pests and diseases include parasitic insects, spiders, parasitic nematodes, birds, toads and frogs, predatory ground beetles and bacteria.

A second form of biological control is that used in enclosed cultivation in greenhouse and glasshouse systems. Rather than encouraging a whole suite of native predators, usually only one predator is actively released into a smaller, enclosed area. A number of firms now sell biological controls for greenhouses and the predators arrive through the post in a small tube or packet. These are available both to the small gardener with a multipurpose greenhouse and to the market gardener or fruit-grower with large glasshouses. For example, a white fly infestation on plants can be controlled by releasing a parasitic wasp called *Encarsia* into the greenhouse.

Advantages of biological pest control

The main advantage of biological pest control is that it avoids the use of chemical sprays. These may be damaging to humans – possibly adding to asthma sufferers' problems. Chemical sprays are certainly damaging to the pest, but also to many other harmless and useful animals. Aquatic organisms close to areas being sprayed are especially susceptible if the pesticide accidentally gets into the water system.

In fact, pesticides are sometimes so damaging to predators that they may even allow the pest to increase! If you look at *figure 2.10* you can see the effect of spraying DDT on a crop of brassicas (e.g. cabbages and Brussels sprouts) in an attempt to control the cabbage white butterfly. After three lots of spraying, more butterfly eggs were found on the crop than in an unsprayed control area. The soil-dwelling predators – beetles and harvestmen – of the cabbage white butterfly, which acted as a natural biological control, had been killed by long-lasting poisonous DDT residues in the soil.

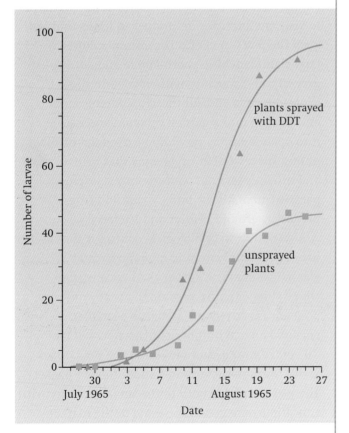

● **Figure 2.10** Graph showing the number of cabbage white butterfly larvae on 64 brassica plants. Half the plants were sprayed with DDT on 6 July and 20 August 1964, and again on 28 July 1965.

On the sprayed crop, 70% of the eggs laid by cabbage white butterflies survived, while only 40% survived on the unsprayed crop, because the predators were still there to eat the eggs. DDT use is now restricted because of its harmful effects on wildlife (see pages 29–30), but even replacement insecticides may have a similar effect. In other words, in some instances it is not only better for the environment but may also be better and cheaper for the farmer not to resort to pesticides.

Sometimes overuse of pesticides leads to the selection of pests that are resistant to many chemical pesticides. Under these circumstances biological control may be the only alternative solution for keeping the pest numbers down.

SAQ 2.4

Give two reasons why farmers who rely on pesticides may need to use ever-increasing amounts of them.

Disadvantages of biological pest control

In open fields there may be quite a time lag between ceasing to use chemicals as pesticides and the build-up of the natural predators of the pests. This is because the natural fauna may be very depleted both in terms of abundance and number of species, so the food web needs time to develop before maximum efficiency is reached.

A related problem is the use of biological control in small areas of land surrounded by intensively farmed land where pesticides are still used. Predators normally range over a wider area than their prey, so the build-up of viable populations of predators in the control area will be constantly hampered by the effect of pesticides in the adjacent areas.

In enclosed crop-growing sites, specific biological control species may have to be bought and released. Monoculture crops, such as tomatoes and aubergines, may not support a long-term viable community so the predator species may die out and have to be reintroduced a number of times during crop growth and maturation.

Using an imported predator in a glasshouse runs the risk that the biological control species may escape or mutate to attack another organism.

If the pest is an introduced species, and has become a pest because no predators are native to the growing area, then the introduction of a non-native predator may be the only alternative to chemicals, even though this constitutes a significant risk to wildlife.

One salutary example occurred on the islands of Polynesia, which had many endemic snails in the genus *Partula*. Here the giant African land snail (*Achatina*) was introduced in the 1960s as a source of human food. It escaped from captivity and ran riot in the native vegetation and crops. It was decided to introduce a small predator snail,

called *Euglandina*, to kill the giant snails. You can of course guess what happened. The introduced predator, the intended biological control agent, found the little native *Partula* species much tastier (or easier to catch and kill) and wiped out about 40 species, most of which are now extinct in their native habitat. Luckily, living specimens of most species were rescued but they now live only in captivity in plastic lunch boxes in the London Zoo and other zoos around the world. The giant land snail continues to munch its way happily across the islands!

SUMMARY

◆ Burning, grazing and mowing can prevent a succession from reaching a climax community, resulting instead in a deflected succession such as grassland.

◆ In intercropping a farmer grows two or more crops in the same field at the same time.

◆ Intercropping can result in increased yields and can conserve soils. It is especially common in tropical countries with year-round growing seasons. However, it can be labour intensive.

◆ Intensive farming relies on the addition of significant amounts of fertiliser. Extensive farming does not and so is more sustainable.

◆ Intensive farming has led to increasing amounts of farm waste and to the destruction of hedgerows. It is also associated in some regions with the reclamation of land from the sea.

◆ Organic farmers avoid artificial pesticides and fertilisers. Organic farming is growing in popularity in industrialised countries though whether it is advantageous for the environment and for consumers is controversial.

◆ Legumes are used for crop rotation as their symbiotic nitrogen-fixing bacteria help fertilise the soil.

◆ Biological pest control can help reduce the use of pesticides but can go spectacularly wrong.

Questions

1 Explain, and illustrate with examples, how deflected successions can arise.

2 Describe how intercropping and crop rotation with legumes can be used in farming.

3 Compare and contrast intensive and extensive farming.

4 Explain what is meant by organic farming and discuss whether it is advantageous or not.

5 Describe the principles behind biological pest control and discuss the implications of its use for a farmer.

Pollution

Introduction

Environmental pollution results from human activity causing the release of substances that should not be there or the build-up of substances to unnatural and damaging levels. The pollutant can be released into water, onto land or into the air, and the harmful effect can be very localised or global in extent. Pollution is usually defined (as here) as the result of human activity. Many substances we consider pollutants – such as carbon dioxide, heavy metals and radioactive ores – occur naturally but at lower concentrations than as a result of human activity.

The earliest global pollution found so far has been detected in the Greenland ice sheet as trapped airborne particles of heavy metals about 4000–3000 years old. Greenland was a long way from any sites of active smelting. The effects of heavy metals such as lead and copper around the actual sites of smelting and casting in Bronze Age China and Roman Europe must have been

substantial, as early processing methods were very inefficient.

With increasing industrialisation, pollution became an ever-increasing problem, as a result of the extraction of raw materials and the processing and disposal of waste products (see also pages 30–31 and 45–48). Intensive farming methods (pages 28–30 and 14–17) and everyday domestic life (pages 49–51) cause pollution too. Most of us use electricity, prefer inexpensive, pest-free food, use transport, create personal and household waste, buy plastic and metal products and so on. All such activities produce pollution somewhere in the world.

Water pollution

Aquatic ecosystems

Seventy percent of the Earth's surface is ocean. Water evaporates from the oceans and rises from vegetation on land by evapotranspiration. The atmospheric water vapour condenses into tiny water droplets, which we see as clouds, mists and fog. High clouds are very cold and snow or hail forms in them, which falls when it gets too heavy to be held up by rising currents of air. Usually this melts as it falls through warmer air and lands as rain. How much rain falls in a year and where determines the natural vegetation in an area – from desert to tropical forest.

Excess surface water drains into freshwater stream systems, carrying with it sand, silt and clay particles, as well as dissolved minerals, nutrients from the soil and plant debris. The dissolved minerals provide nutrients for algae that coat the pebbles or stones and are grazed by water snails and fly larvae (figure 3.1). These, in turn, are eaten by leeches, flatworms, carnivorous insect larvae and fish. In slow-moving rivers, the sand and silt settles out of the water to give more silty and muddy bottoms. This is a better substrate for aquatic plants to root and different invertebrates (such as oligochaete worms and bivalve molluscs) live in the mud. Healthy streams and rivers have high biodiversity.

Lakes form where the flow of water is blocked. In the UK, the lakes in the Lake District formed when the valley glaciers melted after the last Ice Age, about 12 000–10 000 years ago, and left great

● **Figure 3.1** Invertebrates in the River Itchen, Hampshire, include the ramshorn snail, freshwater shrimps, water boatmen, a caddis larva and a dragonfly nymph. Such a variety indicates the water is unpolluted.

ridges of debris across the ends of the valleys. Some lakes are artificial: reservoirs created by damming rivers for hydroelectric schemes or water storage, or for recreation such as sailing and fishing, or even for landscape design. Shallow lakes where sunlight reaches the bottom are often very diverse, with freshwater sponges, rooted aquatics and a whole mix of invertebrates, fish and associated birds such as ducks and divers. Deep lakes only have rooted vegetation around their edges and floating or suspended primary producers on the main body of the lake.

All waterways are at risk from damage by over-enthusiastic management: tidying up of stream banks, removing meanders and dredging. There is an ever-increasing demand for the extraction of water for domestic use (see pages 48–49), which may reduce water flow too much. Waterways are also used as dumps for our rubbish. This includes organic matter (especially sewage), toxins (including agricultural pesticides and industrial waste) and general debris from urban waste. The great rivers of Europe, such as the Rhine, are now heavily polluted and the noxious concoction of organic and chemical waste flows out into the North Sea and elsewhere to pollute the marine environment as well.

Eutrophication

Most lakes are naturally nutrient poor, especially when young, and are described as **oligotrophic lakes**. There is a tendency for the nutrient content of a lake to rise over hundreds of years as the rivers feeding it deliver nutrients: a process known as **natural eutrophication**. These old lakes and other naturally richer lakes (such as tend to occur where rivers flow over highly fertile soils) are naturally eutrophic lakes.

The most common risk to freshwater systems is now **anthropogenic eutrophication** (also known as **cultural eutrophication**) that is nutrient enrichment due to certain types of pollution. Such eutrophication occurs when excess nitrates, phosphates and organic matter get into the water system. About 80% of water pollution is from domestic sewage and waste from industry with 20% being from agriculture, including fertilisers and livestock slurry. Encouragingly, in most industrialised countries raw sewage release is decreasing as sewage treatment improves (see page 49). Eutrophication encourages rapid increases in populations of algae, diatoms, cyanobacteria and some plants such as Canadian pondweed, duckweed (*Lemna*) and yellow water lily. Usually a few species become dominant and other species are lost, resulting in reduced biodiversity. The waterway may become clogged (*figure 3.2*) and the loss of habitat diversity means that animal biodiversity suffers too. Some cyanobacteria are highly toxic to animals using the water to drink.

Biochemical oxygen demand

A rise in organic matter due to pollution from raw sewage, food processing, abattoirs, agricultural slurry or domestic waste is usually accompanied by eutrophication. This encourages massive rises in aerobic bacterial populations, which use up the oxygen in the water as they feed on the organic matter. Most organisms normally found in unpolluted water are killed by this lack of oxygen. Only a few species (such as chironomid larvae and oligochaete worms) thrive as they can tolerate low oxygen levels and feed on the bacteria in the water. If the input of organic matter pollution ceases, oxygen levels eventually rise and the normal fauna recolonise.

● **Figure 3.2** Algal blooms clogging the New Bedford River (Hundred Foot Drain), Cambridgeshire.

The fact that oxygen is required in the decomposition of the organic matter can be used as a measure of how polluted the water is. A sample of water is taken and kept dark (to prevent photosynthesis) for 5 days at 20 °C. The amount of oxygen used up by the microorganisms in breaking down the organic matter during the test period is called the **biochemical oxygen demand** (also sometimes known as the **biological oxygen demand**) or **BOD** and is measured in mg of oxygen per dm^3 per 5 days. If a sample has a very high organic matter content it can be diluted by a known amount and a subsample tested. The actual BOD of the original sample can then be calculated by knowing by how much it was diluted. *Table 3.1* shows the BOD of some organic pollutants.

SAQ 3.1

Explain how anthropogenic eutrophication can lead to the loss of certain species from aquatic habitats.

Indicator species of water pollution

Water pollution can be monitored in two ways. One is by analysis of water to determine the biochemical oxygen demand (BOD) and hence the levels of organic compounds, or by using chemical reagents to assess the absolute levels of various pollutants, such as heavy metals, nitrates (NO_3^-) and phosphates (PO_4^{3-}). The other method is to

Substance	BOD (mg dm^{-3})
milk	140 000
concentrated silage effluent	30 000–80 000
brewer's grain effluent	30 000–50 000
pig slurry	20 000–30 000
cattle slurry	10 000–20 000
liquid sewage sludge	10 000–20 000
dairy parlour and yard washings	1000–2000
raw domestic sewage	300–400
treated sewage	20–60
unpolluted river water	< 5

● **Table 3.1** Biochemical oxygen demand for various organic pollutants. Remember that pollutants such as slurry or effluent will be diluted when they enter an aquatic system; these figures are for the pollutants before they enter a river.

use **indicator species**, which relies on an understanding of the tolerance levels of different species to pollution. The idea is that by

Families		Score
• Siphlonuridae, Heptageniidae, Leptophlebiidae, Ephemerellidae, Potamanthidae, Ephemeridae	(mayflies)	
• Taeniopterygidae, Leuctridae, Capniidae, Perlodidae, Perlidae, Chloroperlidae	(stoneflies)	
• Aphelocheiridae	(beetles)	10
• Phryganeidae, Molannidae, Beraeidae, Odontoceridae, Leptoceridae, Goeridae, Lepidostomatidae, Brachycentridae, Sericostomatidae	(caddis-flies)	
• Astacidae	(crayfish)	
• Lestidae, Agriidae, Gomphidae, Cordulegasteridae, Aeshnidae, Corduliidae, Libellulidae	(dragonflies)	8
• Psychomyiidae, Philopotamidae	(net-spinning caddis-flies)	
• Caenidae	(mayflies)	
• Nemouridae	(stoneflies)	7
• Rhyacophilidae, Polycentropodidae, Limnephilidae	(net-spinning caddis-flies)	
• Neritidae, Viviparidae, Ancylidae	(snails)	
• Hydroptilidae	(caddis-flies)	
• Unionidae	(bivalve molluscs)	6
• Corophiidae, Gammaridae	(crustacea)	
• Platycnemididae, Coenagriidae	(dragonflies)	
• Mesovelidae, Hydrometridae, Gerridae, Nepidae, Naucoridae, Notonectidae, Pleidae, Corixidae	(bugs)	
• Haliplidae, Hygrobiidae, Dytiscidae, Gyrinidae, Hydrophilidae, Clambidae, Helodidae, Dryopidae, Elminthidae, Crysomelidae, Curculionidae	(beetles)	5
• Hydropsychidae	(caddis-flies)	
• Tipulidae, Simuliidae	(dipteran flies)	
• Planariidae, Dendrocoelidae	(triclads)	
• Baetidae	(mayflies)	
• Sialidae	(alderfly)	4
• Piscicolidae	(leeches)	
• Valvatidae, Hydrobiidae, Lymnaeidae, Physidae, Planorbidae, Sphaeriidae	(snails, bivalves)	
• Glossiphoniidae, Hirudidae, Erpobdellidae	(leeches)	3
• Asellidae	(crustacea)	
• Chironomidae	(diptera)	2
• Oligochaeta (whole class)	(worms)	1

● **Table 3.2** The invertebrate list for monitoring pollution in streams and rivers. The score is calculated as the *average* score for all families found in the waterway. For example if a river contains families which score 4, 5, 5, 8, 10 and 10 then the river scores 42/6 = 7. The lower the score, the more polluted the river.

observing which organisms are present and which are absent from a habitat the level of pollution can be estimated.

These two methods complement each other. Chemical methods and the determination of BOD provide an instantaneous measure of pollutants. Indicator species, on the other hand, provide a *summary* of the recent history of the environment. For example, suppose that chemical reagents reveal low levels of nitrates and phosphates while indicator species suggest high levels of pollution. The resolution of this apparent paradox might be that there was a recent surge of nitrates and phosphates, perhaps from fertiliser or sewage run-off. Though the surge itself may be over within weeks, the biological effects may last a year or more.

Usually it is the *absence* of a group of indicator species that provides evidence for pollution. However some species are known to grow where there has been pollution. Both the nettle (*Urtica dioica*) and Indian balsam (*Impatiens glandulifera*) are flowering plants that grow where nutrient levels are very high. Nettles grow around abandoned dwellings and balsam grows along stream banks polluted with sewage.

Invertebrates can be used as biological indicators to detect the organic pollution of water systems (*figure 3.1*). The decrease in oxygen content caused by aerobic bacteria as they decompose organic matter such as sewage causes the death of many types of invertebrates living in the stream or river.

The Trent River Authority first devised a recording system for monitoring the pollution of watercourses in 1964. *Table 3.2* shows the score chart of the Biological Monitoring Working Party. In this system, points are allocated according to whether or not **key groups** of invertebrates are present. Note that the invertebrates need only be identified to family level (there are illustrated keys available to aid identification). As you can see, the two families that thrive in polluted waters, chironomids and oligochaete worms, are at the bottom of the table with the lowest scores. They are found even in highly polluted streams and rivers with very low levels of dissolved oxygen (< 10% saturation). At the other end of the scale, most mayfly and stonefly nymphs can only survive in waters with high levels of dissolved oxygen (> 80% saturation). Periodic surveys of water courses in England and Wales classify streams and rivers on the basis of their dissolved oxygen concentrations, ammonia concentrations, ability to support fish and invertebrate presence as scored in *table 3.2*.

Aquatic plants release oxygen during photosynthesis so they are generally only affected by severe oxygen depletion. However, where sewage pollution is persistent, few plants can grow because of the dense coverings of algae or cyanobacteria, which block out the light (*figure 3.2*). Usually when invertebrates die off, the plants still appear healthy. However, plants are much more sensitive to toxins such as heavy metals and chemical herbicides than are invertebrates. Where such pollution is slight, all that may show is a yellowing of leaves or fewer new growing shoots. Plant death in a river or stream occurs close to the source of the pollution where the toxins are most concentrated, while maximum invertebrate death typically occurs between one and two kilometres downstream where the organic matter has been carried by the current and the decomposers have had time to multiply. Thus aquatic plants and invertebrates complement each other as biological indicators.

SAQ 3.2

Explain why the use of biochemical oxygen demand and indicator species may give different measures of water pollution.

SAQ 3.3

Suppose a river sample contains only the families Piscicolidae, Planorbidae, Hirudidae, Asellidae and Chironomidae. From *table 3.2*, compute the Biological Monitoring Working Party pollution score.

Pesticides

Most of our synthetic pesticides have been developed since the 1940s and are used in tandem with chemical fertilisers in intensive farming systems. This is illustrated in the global use of pesticides, which is much higher in North America, Japan and Europe than in the less intensively farmed parts of the world (*figure 3.3*). Unless a farmer follows the path of organic production and biological pest control (see pages 18 and 21), the use of pesticides is necessary in an intensive farming regime to prevent damage to crops while they are growing, and to give a longer shelf life to fruits and vegetables by reducing decay from surface microorganisms. Pesticides are also used to reduce infections in

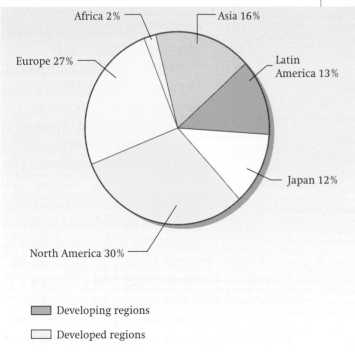

● **Figure 3.3** Pesticide sales in 1994 as percentages of the global total.

farm animals and therefore improve their standard of living. Farming is subject to market forces, including economic ones, and pesticides are now a part of that. In real terms, farming incomes in the UK more than halved from the 1970s to the 1990s and the occurrence of BSE (mad cow disease) in cattle only made this worse. Employment in agriculture continues to fall and suicide rates for farmers remain far above the national average.

Pesticides include herbicides (used against weeds), fungicides (which kill fungi such as mildews and rusts) and insecticides (to kill insects). By their very nature pesticides are intended to kill organisms, so it is not surprising that their use can cause environmental and health problems. Even in the right place a pesticide is bound to interfere with food webs by killing one or more species in the area. A pesticide in the wrong place can have a devastating effect on an ecosystem. Pesticide use undoubtedly poses a risk to human health. Anything from a headache and rash to asthma, allergies, damage to the immune system and nervous disorders have been blamed on pesticide sprays, residues on produce and organophosphate sheep dips. Even though most pesticides are used in Europe, America and Japan (*figure 3.3*), poisoning incidents are worst in developing countries where safety procedures are not as thorough.

Many **herbicides** break down rapidly, being **biodegradable**, and are only poisonous to animals when absorbed or ingested at high concentrations. Some new herbicides are selective, designed to kill only the broad-leaved plants in a grain crop or the grasses in a flower bed. Herbicide use has been responsible for a great reduction in the variety and number of plants seen on UK farmlands. Even poppies are uncommon in many parts of the country, and several species that were serious agricultural weeds 50 years ago are now national rarities. These include the beautiful corncockle (*Agrostemma githago*) with its large purple flowers and shepherd's-needle (*Scandix pecten-veneris*) with its delicate white petals and long, needle-like fruits.

Certain inorganic chemicals have long been used as **fungicides**. Copper salts have been employed to protect grapevines against fungi for over 100 years. More recently a number of carbon-based fungicides, such as zineb and benomyl, have been developed. Fungicides are not known to cause many ecological problems, but that may be due to our lack of understanding of the role of fungi in ecosystems.

Substances used as **insecticides** include pyrethroids, organochlorines, organophosphates and carbamates. Organophosphates and carbamates are particularly toxic. Insecticides tend to be the most widely used pesticides in domestic situations (moth, carpet-beetle and flea killers) as well as in forestry, food storage, horticulture and agriculture.

A common problem with many insecticides is that as well as killing the intended pest, known as the **target species**, they often kill useful pollinating insects, or even predators and parasites of the target species, as described on page 22. A farmer may become locked into an expensive cycle, being forced to spray more frequently and more extensively because the natural predators of the target species have been wiped out. This is where organic farming (see pages 18–20) tries to reset the balance by promoting healthy populations of predators to control target species. More recently pheromones, insect growth regulators and other hormones have been developed which disrupt aspects of the target species' life cycle from reproduction to moulting. These approaches are more pest specific and may be the way forward to controlling pests with minimal damage to the environment.

A second problem is that the target species may evolve *resistance* to the insecticide. The farmer could respond by using increased dosages. However, switching to a different class of insecticide for a couple of years may be a better strategy. The use of natural poisons as pesticides may cause unexpected problems to wildlife. For example, some pesticides mimic the toxins spiders use to catch their prey. If insects become resistant to these, this could be disastrous for the spiders!

A third problem with some insecticides is that they can become concentrated up food chains. **DDT**, first used in 1939 to kill lice and mosquitoes, and other related organochlorines last for 10–25 years in the environment. They are much more soluble in fat than in water so once ingested they remain in the fatty tissues of animals rather than

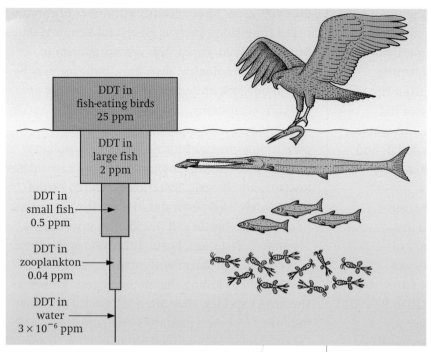

● **Figure 3.4** An example of how DDT concentrations increase up the trophic levels of an estuarine food chain.

being excreted. When herbivores that have grazed on plants sprayed with DDT are eaten by secondary consumers and so on up the food chain, very high concentrations of DDT build up in the top carnivores (*figure 3.4*). (If you want to know what DDT stands for it is dichlorodiphenyltrichloroethane!)

Accumulation of DDT and other organochlorines in animals can be dangerous. In the 1950s the number of peregrine falcons in Europe began to fall and halved over the next twenty years. Research showed that the use of DDT as an insecticide and aldrin and dieldrin as seed dressings eaten by pigeons led to the accumulation of organochlorine residues within the falcons. These concentrated organochlorines caused the birds to lay eggs with thinner shells. As a result, the eggs were more likely to break before hatching. Eventually the British and other governments introduced restrictions on the use of organochlorine insecticides. By the late 1980s, peregrine falcon numbers were back to their former levels.

Other toxins

Other long-lasting chemical toxins released into the environment include about 200 different polychlorinated biphenyls (**PCBs**), first used in the US in 1929. PCBs conduct heat but not electricity, so they were widely used in industry as coolants and as electrical insulators. They were also used in the manufacture of paints, inks and plastics. Their polluting effects were first noticed in the 1960s and they were banned in the 1970s. PCBs have a similar effect to DDT in that they are long lasting in the environment and concentrate in lipids (fatty tissues).

PCBs are now widespread in sediments and water. They have contaminated the oceans and directly enter the bodies of marine organisms from the sea water. They are especially concentrated in the lipids of many marine organisms from the tiniest invertebrates and shellfish to vertebrates including fish, whales and seals. The tissues of seabirds and other animals with a largely fish diet also have high concentrations of PCBs.

PCBs cause eggshell thinning in birds and also interfere with mammalian reproduction, damage the immune system and cause cancer. It is thought that PCBs have contributed to mass deaths of marine mammals, including whales and dolphins, by causing them stress and weakening their immune systems, making them susceptible to toxins in the water or viral attack. Since 1988, 20 000 seals (nearly half the population) in the North Sea and surrounding waters, died of viral infections that are thought to have been enhanced by PCB poisoning. Pregnant women exposed to PCBs give birth to children who have problems with memory, lowered intelligence, poor growth and damaged immune systems. People with a diet high in fish, shellfish and marine mammals are particularly at risk of PCB poisoning: Inuit nursing mothers have been found with five times more PCBs in their milk than southern Canadians.

Heavy metals are also pollutants if they become concentrated in water systems or soils. As was noted on page 7, pollution due to the smelting of ores for copper, iron, zinc, tin and lead has been with us for thousands of years. Like many substances we have already mentioned, heavy metal pollution has increased hugely since the industrial revolution. In the environment the heaviest concentrations occur on spoil heaps and mine wastes. Where tips have been left undisturbed, plants able to grow in the presence of particular metals eventually colonise and leave similarly tolerant offspring. Thus in the parts of the Yorkshire Dales and Derbyshire where abandoned lead mines occur, the pretty flower known locally as leadwort (*Minuartia verna*) grows in abundance (*figure 3.5*). Any environmentalist wishing to landscape a recent spoil heap would do well to collect seed from the vegetation on an old colonised tip, as the seed will have a better chance of containing metal-tolerant genes than a commercial mix would.

High concentrations of heavy metals are very toxic to animals, causing developmental defects, cancers, kidney failure and immune system failure. Lead, once commonly put in paints and petrol and used for water pipes, is especially toxic, causing autoimmune problems (resulting in arthritis and kidney failure) and damage to internal organs as well as a reduction in IQ and behavioural problems. Lead is so potent that we may all be suffering from some degree of lead poisoning, though since the introduction of

● **Figure 3.5** Leadwort (*Minuartia verna*) growing on the spoil from lead mining in Derbyshire.

lead-free petrol and paints in the UK this risk is certainly less than our parents had!

In gold-mining areas, large quantities of mercury are used to extract the gold. It has become a serious pollutant in areas of the Amazon basin. The worst form of mercury poisoning occurs where the mercury forms part of a carbon-based compound. Children in affected areas may be born with horrific deformities. A serious incident of mercury poisoning occurred around Minamata Bay, Japan, in the 1950s when a local chemical plant released methyl mercury into the river. This entered the marine food chains and when the local people ate shellfish and fish from the bay the mercury poisoning killed or disabled over 1000 people during the following 20 years.

Air pollution

The global problem

Atmospheric pollution is very difficult to control. Because winds know no international borders, neither does atmospheric pollution and this, above all, makes such pollution a global concern. As a result there has been far more co-operation and global legislation for air pollution than for any other type of pollution. The rest of this chapter deals with the three main forms of atmospheric pollution. The first, acid rain, is the most localised, usually only affecting the region in which the pollutant was released. However, the other two are global in their consequences – the ozone hole and global warming – and as such require worldwide co-operation to control.

Acid rain

Acid rain is the collective name given to a number of processes, all of which involve the deposition of acidic gases from the atmosphere (*figure 3.6*). Most deposition is indeed in rain or mist, though some direct, so-called **dry deposition**, occurs without rainwater acting as a vehicle.

Natural, unpolluted rain has a pH of about 5.6, because atmospheric carbon dioxide dissolves in it to form the mildly acidic carbonic acid. However, in Britain, the rest of Europe and North America, rainwater often has a pH of between 4 and 4.5,

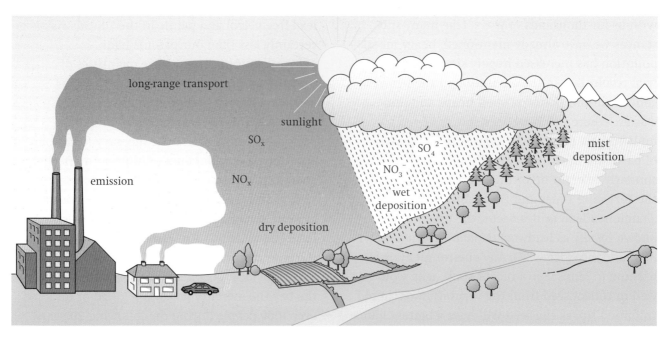

● **Figure 3.6** The main gases involved in the formation of acid rain are sulphur oxides (SO$_x$) and nitrogen oxides (NO$_x$). Acid deposition is particularly important in areas covered by mist for long periods of time.

and sometimes much lower than this. A rainstorm at Pitlochry in Scotland on 10 April 1974 had a pH of 2.4 – more acidic than vinegar! This increased acidity is due to the presence of nitrogen oxides (NO$_x$) and sulphur oxides (SO$_x$), which dissolve in rainwater to give nitric acid and sulphuric acid.

Acid rain results from the combustion of fossil fuels in power stations (coal, oil or gas), vehicles (petrol) and metal smelting plants. Not all these sources are equally to blame. Coals with a high sulphur content are particularly harmful. Many environmentalists blame acid rain for much of the damage seen in trees in European and North American forests. Scientists employed by the power generation industry are generally more cautious in their conclusions. Certainly, many lichens cannot tolerate high SO$_x$ levels.

Both trees and lichens live for a long time, which may explain their susceptibility, as they would suffer accumulated damage. The most noticeable symptom of acid rain in trees is crown dieback, where the top of the tree dies. In some countries, particularly at high altitudes and at the edges of forests, large areas are covered with dead or dying trees. Conifers seem particularly at risk: evergreen conifers such as pines and firs renew only a portion of their leaves each year, so each leaf has four or five years of exposure to the

atmosphere. The leaves of deciduous trees and herbaceous plants live only a few months and in winter there are no leaves to intercept the acid rain. In spring when leaves are tender, damage may be quite bad, but only one season's growth is damaged. Most trees can grow replacement leaves, but the extra energy used to grow them may lead to failure to reproduce and increased susceptibility to disease, pests, drought or frosts. Acid rain has also been implicated in lack of breeding success in a number of birds in the Netherlands.

Acid rain also affects freshwater ecosystems. Between the 1960s and 1980s, many Scandinavian and Scottish lakes lost large numbers of their fish and other fauna. This correlated with increasing acidification of the lakes. The situation is most severe in lakes on granite rocks: fresh water on limestone is much better at buffering the acid. Fish embryos are damaged and killed in water with a pH below 5.5, and adult reproduction is also affected. Increased acidity in rivers also disrupts the homing instincts of salmon, which return to their own rivers to spawn. The eggs and young (fry) of fish are directly affected by low pH.

An indirect effect of lower pH is the increase in metal ions such as aluminium, copper, nickel, zinc and mercury, leached out of the soil and into the streams by the acid rain. At low pH more aluminium (present in soil clay) can exist in solution. Aluminium is known to be toxic and some plant and fish species are particularly susceptible. Aluminium interferes with the regulation of gill permeability by calcium. As a result, sodium is lost and the gill surfaces clog with mucus, causing respiratory stress. Aluminium may also lower calcium uptake, leading to poor bone structure and inter-fering with egg production. High aluminium concentrations in water can even lead to adult fish death. Salmon and minnows are much more sensitive to the effects of acid rain than are pike or eels. Calcium uptake by crustaceans and molluscs is also interfered with: without calcium they cannot manufacture their exoskeletons or shells.

How can the problems of acid rain be reversed? Some success has been achieved at raising the pH of a few lakes by adding large amounts of calcium carbonate (limestone). However, the only long-term solution is to reduce emissions of sulphur and nitrogen oxides. Car exhaust fumes can be cleaned up with catalytic converters. Sulphur dioxide emissions from power stations and smelting plants can be reduced using sulphur dioxide scrubbers. Unfortunately, these scrubbers require large amounts of limestone, which is both expensive and requires extensive quarrying. The British power industry now uses natural gas, oil and imported low-sulphur coal, which helps, though at the expense of the British coal-mining industry. New power stations and industrial plants are being built with improved systems for cleaning the emissions. In Europe, trends indicate that the 1990 levels of acid rain emissions will have halved by 2010. However, for countries such as India and China, coal is the major fuel in power stations and clean-ing measures are expensive (*figure 3.7*). In Asia, acid emissions are set to triple between 1990 and 2010.

● **Figure 3.7** Industrial pollution in Liaoning Province, China.

Indicator species of airborne pollution

Lichens seem particularly sensitive to sulphur dioxide and therefore acid rain. They rely on rain-fall for their water supply and are slow growing, but long lived. The species present and the size and condition of each lichen can indicate long- or short-term pollution and even recovery if substan-tial new growth is found. Only a small number of species of lichen can survive in heavily polluted air.

In a classic study in the late 1960s, D. L. Hawksworth and F. Rose classified different species of lichens into ten groups, which they called zones. Zone 10 contained lichens that were particularly sensitive to atmospheric sulphur dioxide (SO_2). Lichens in zone 9 could tolerate mean levels of winter sulphur dioxide deposition of up to $30\,\mu g\,m^{-3}$. Lichens in zone 8 could tolerate levels of between 30 and $35\,\mu g\,m^{-3}$, and so on. The only lichens that could tolerate mean winter sulphur dioxide deposition levels of $150–170\,\mu g\,m^{-3}$ were *Lecanora conizaeoides* and *L. expallens*. Zone 1 contained no lichens, only the green alga *Pleurococcus viridis*. Zone 0 contained neither lichens nor algae. *Figure 3.8* shows the distribution of these lichen zones in England and Wales. As you might expect, the higher zones are found only in rural areas where the air contains the least pollutants.

In tropical vegetation, plants that grow attached to trees, and therefore obtain all their

SAQ 3.4
List five harmful consequences of acid rain.

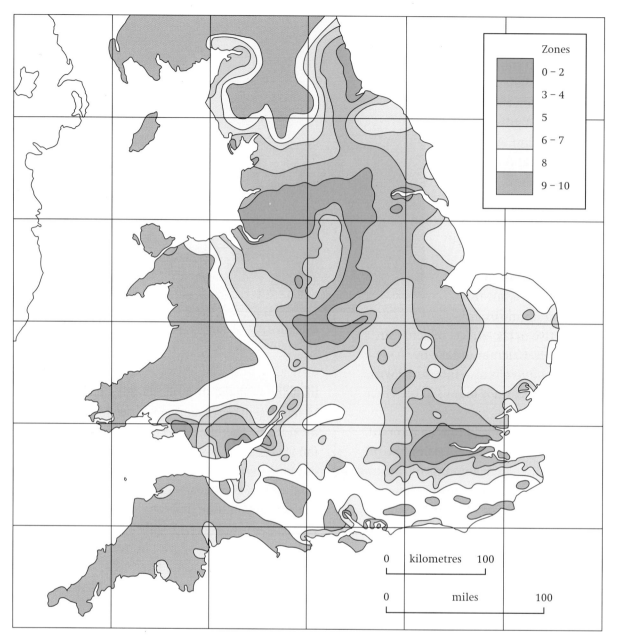

● **Figure 3.8** Distribution of lichen zones in England and Wales in the late 1960s as determined by D. L. Hawksworth and F. Rose. Zone 10 has the most species of lichen, Zone 0 none.

water from rainfall, are called epiphytes (*figure 6.6 on page 71*). These too are particularly sensitive to air pollution and make good indicator species. Such epiphytes include orchids and bromeliads.

The ozone hole

The importance of ozone

Ozone, O_3, is a very important component of the atmosphere. Close to the ground, ozone is produced by the action of light on exhaust fumes and so concentrates where traffic is heavy. Here it is a pollutant: it corrodes metals, inhibits plant growth and irritates the lungs and throat. At high levels, 15–50 km above the Earth's surface, in the stratosphere, it plays a crucial role in maintaining healthy life as it intercepts much of the Sun's ultraviolet (UV) radiation that would otherwise reach the Earth. Excess UV radiation damages the DNA (deoxyribonucleic acid) in cells and increases mutation rates. It also reduces metabolism in plants and algae, and increases the occurrence of skin cancers and cataracts in animals (including humans). It may also damage the immune system. The extent of the damage to natural ecosystems is really unknown, but there is some evidence that UV light causes high mortality in juvenile amphibians and fish. Algae are at the base of marine food webs, so damage to these – especially around Antarctica – could cause long-lasting damage to marine ecosystems.

In the stratosphere, ozone is formed from oxygen in the presence of sunlight (a photochemical reaction). Most ozone, as a consequence, forms above the tropics where the sunlight is strongest, and no ozone forms over whichever pole is in darkness. During the mid-1980s measurements above Antarctica showed a significant decrease in the amount of ozone there. By the beginning of the 1990s it had become a large hole. More recently, the same phenomenon has been observed above the Arctic producing seasonal holes in the ozone layer. The ozone layer at lower latitudes is also thinner due to ozone depletion, and therefore even in Britain it is no longer advisable to tan without a sun filter to block the increased UV radiation.

Chlorofluorocarbons

There are several chemicals containing chlorine or bromine responsible for the thinning of the ozone layer. They are called halocarbons and include **chlorofluorocarbons (CFCs)** (*figure 3.9*), although nitrous oxide (N_2O) and methane are also culprits. The problem is worst in winter. This is because at very low temperatures the CFCs accumulate in the clouds. When the polar area is hit again by sunlight in spring, a photochemical reaction is triggered, which breaks down the CFCs to release 'free radical' (highly reactive) chlorine atoms. The chlorine atoms then react with ozone thus:

$$Cl\cdot + O_3 \rightarrow ClO\cdot + O_2$$

The $ClO\cdot$ then reacts with other atmospheric components. In the

stratosphere this is usually an oxygen atom:

$$ClO\cdot + O \rightarrow Cl\cdot + O_2$$

The 'dots' after Cl and ClO indicate that they are 'free radicals'.

If you look closely at these two equations you will see that a molecule of ozone is destroyed *without* the chlorine atom being used up. It has been calculated that a single CFC molecule can remove hundreds of thousands of ozone molecules.

In the 1970s and 1980s, CFCs were widely used in refrigerators, fire extinguishers, aerosol sprays, solvents, cleaning agents and fast-food packaging. Other halocarbons include the pesticide methyl bromide. Once the hole in the ozone layer was discovered, countries came under great pressure by environmentalists and scientists to act to prevent further damage. An initial convention of 49 countries in Vienna in 1985 led to the signing (in 1987) of the **Montreal Protocol on Substances that Deplete the Ozone Layer**, the first ever big international treaty on the environment. This laid down targets to ensure that fewer CFCs were released into the atmosphere. The aim was to halve the emissions of CFCs between 1986 and 1999. Since 1987, further modifications have been made to the protocol, including the need for much

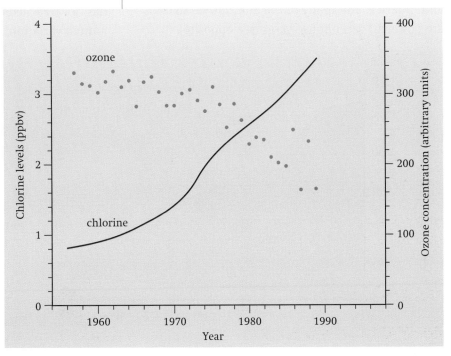

● **Figure 3.9** Changes in global average concentration of chlorine from halocarbons in the troposphere in parts per billion by volume (ppbv) (line) and the total ozone over Antarctica in October of each year (dots).

greater reductions in CFC release. By 1995, 150 countries had signed up. Although some governments have been reluctant to comply, there has been a significant reduction in the use of CFCs (*figure 3.10*).

This is seen as a big success story. The developed nations have co-operated to produce great reductions in CFC release (*figure 3.10*). However, there are still a number of problems which mean success has not yet been achieved. Firstly, CFCs can persist in the stratosphere for 70 years or more, so destruction of ozone will continue, even if no more CFCs are released. Secondly, the Montreal Protocol only applied to developed countries, as many developing countries, like India and China, only agreed to sign up if they could continue to use CFCs until 2010. There is a fund to help countries switch to less ozone-damaging technology that has helped over 100 countries, but many say it is not sufficient, especially as some rich nations have not provided as much money as they promised. Methyl bromide production will not be cut back until 2002, yet bromine is probably responsible for about 15% of ozone loss so far. Bromine is between 40 and 100 times more efficient at destroying ozone than chlorine! To top it all, there is a black market in CFCs in Europe and America, and many of the alternatives to CFCs are powerful greenhouse gases (see opposite).

If the measures to protect the ozone layer fail, the most immediate consequence for humans may be a significant increase in the number of cases of skin cancer. The first countries to suffer will be those that are close to Antarctica, such as Australia. The ultraviolet rays can also damage the eyes. Even the decrease in the ozone layer up to 1999 is estimated to have caused over a quarter of a million extra cases of skin cancer and over 1.5 million cases of cataracts.

Carbon dioxide

The carbon cycle

Carbon dioxide (CO_2) is an odourless, invisible gas that is vital for photosynthesis and occurs naturally in the atmosphere at a concentration of less than 0.05%. Yet it may turn out to be the most serious pollutant of the next 50 years. Why?

Measurements of the carbon dioxide concentration of air bubbles trapped in the ice of Antarctica suggest that from 2500 to about 200 years ago the concentration of carbon dioxide in the atmosphere remained around 270 parts per million (ppm). Since then, the atmospheric concentration of carbon dioxide has been rising at an ever-increasing rate. It has now reached over 360 ppm (*figure 3.11*). The annual variation, seen as the zig-zag line in *figure 3.11* shows that carbon dioxide falls each spring and summer due to uptake by plants as they grow and produce new leaves. It rises again each autumn and winter as the leaves fall and decay, releasing carbon dioxide.

There are two reasons for the overall rise in carbon dioxide. The main one is the global use of **fossil fuels** – coal, oil, gas and peat – as sources of energy. These fossil fuels have been laid down over hundreds of millions of years and act as **sinks** in the carbon cycle. Normally carbon, once trapped in these sinks, rarely escapes. Burning fossil fuel releases this additional carbon as CO_2 in the atmosphere.

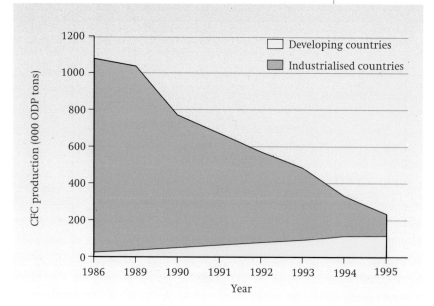

● **Figure 3.10** Global production of CFCs (given in Ozone-Depleting Potential 'ODP' tons) showing a fall in total production but a small rise in CFC production by developing countries.

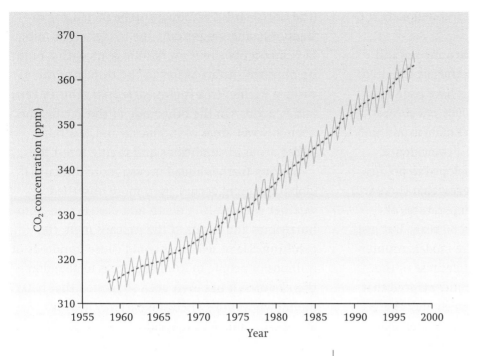

● **Figure 3.11** The atmospheric concentration of CO_2 in parts per million (ppm) measured at monthly intervals in Hawaii showing the annual variation and increasing overall trend. Hawaii, way out in the Pacific Ocean, is the best place to measure the *average* atmospheric CO_2 for the Northern Hemisphere.

The second reason for the increase is the destruction of the world's forests, which removes trees that would otherwise act as carbon reservoirs. Although deforestation creates an increase in atmospheric CO_2, this process is reversible: the regrowth of forests uses up CO_2 by fixing the carbon in wood growth and releasing oxygen. Hence, in principle, the CO_2 is recyclable in living plants: their energy would be a renewable resource if only they were allowed to regrow.

The greenhouse effect

We owe our lives to the **greenhouse effect**, as without it we would be very cold! The presence of our atmosphere increases the surface temperature of the Earth by an average of about 33 °C. The greenhouse effect is so called because carbon dioxide and other atmospheric gases trap warmth around the Earth in much the same way as glass traps heat in a greenhouse. The Sun's energy (we see some as light) travels through the atmosphere and warms the Earth's surface. Some of this heat is radiated back into the atmosphere, where gases

prevent the heat energy escaping from the Earth's atmosphere and into outer space.

In the atmosphere carbon dioxide, methane, water vapour, hydrocarbons, nitrous oxide and chlorofluorocarbons all contribute to the greenhouse effect and have been termed **greenhouse gases** (*figure 3.12*). Some of these are atmospheric pollutants and are completely anthropogenic (of human origin). Others like CO_2 and methane have increased in abundance due to human activity. By increasing carbon dioxide and other atmospheric pollutants, we may be triggering **global warming** by enhancing the natural greenhouse effect of the atmosphere.

Methane is produced from fossil fuels, in rubbish dumps, in swamps, in paddy fields and inside ruminants. As a greenhouse gas it is about ten times more effective than CO_2. Although its concentration in the atmosphere is much less than carbon dioxide (measured in parts per billion, not million), it has risen from about 800 parts per billion by volume (ppbv) to 1720 ppbv in the last 200 years and now contributes about 15%

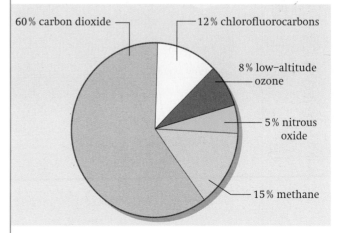

● **Figure 3.12** Pie chart of the greenhouse gases showing their relative contribution to the anthropogenic (human) part of the greenhouse effect.

to the greenhouse effect while carbon dioxide contributes about 60% (*figure 3.12*).

The consequences of global warming are still uncertain. We know that during the last hundred years average world temperatures have risen by over 0.5 °C (*figure 3.13*) and the 1990s saw record-breaking warm years. However, climate is naturally very variable so this may just be a coincidence. Computer models have been developed to predict what will happen next. They suggest that there will be increases in average world temperatures of between 1 and 5 °C over the next 50 years. But just putting extra cloud cover into the models counteracts the predictions of warming. Because of the uncertainty, some scientists are unconvinced that global warming is occurring, even though the increase in greenhouse gases is unquestionable.

What would be the ecological consequences of global warming? Again, we simply do not know for sure. What seems to have happened *already* is that the ocean surface at the equator has become warmer, causing more water to evaporate. The warmer air rises faster than usual, which results in stronger winds that carry the moisture-laden air further from the tropics. Because of this, the tropics receive less rain than usual, whereas in temperate regions floods are more likely. This may be why, over the last 30 years, we seem to have had more droughts than usual in the tropics, and more extremes of weather generally. The extreme weather effect in the Pacific, known as El Niño

(the Christ-child) is thought to be increasing in frequency and magnitude due to global warming. El Niño occurs about every four years with a build-up of warm surface water in the tropics of the eastern Pacific. This causes torrential rains in Peru and Ecuador. On the other side of the Pacific, the normally wet areas of Indonesia and Australia suffer drought conditions and raging forest fires.

Looking further ahead is even more difficult. If global warming occurs, even more unsettled weather will result in death and destruction from hurricanes and floods. If the ice caps melt, the resulting rise in sea levels could cause hundreds of millions of people in low-lying areas to abandon their homes. It has even been suggested that polar meltdown would switch the path of the Gulf Stream, causing a much *colder* climate locally in the North Atlantic including the UK.

The melting of the ice caps and a warmer climate would have profound consequences for biodiversity. As someone put it, 'Can polar bears tread water?' The British charity Plantlife has carried out a detailed assessment of the likely effects of global warming on the British flora. Some plants might benefit. Several of our most rare and beautiful orchids, for example, would probably increase northwards in range. On the other hand, many plants adapted to colder conditions would probably suffer. Some of the possible consequences are surprising. Bluebells, for example, rely on cool spring weather which allows them to grow before other, larger plants come into leaf. It had been supposed that warmer springs might lead to the loss of bluebells from Britain. However, in the very early spring of 1999, the bluebells came out even earlier and still beat the trees into leaf. The complexity of ecosystems makes it very difficult to predict how changes in climate will affect biodiversity.

What we probably *can* predict is that global warming will result in the need for species to move to new

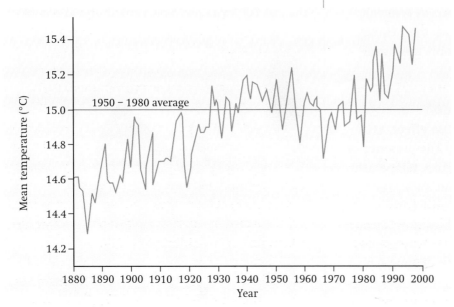

● **Figure 3.13** Mean annual global temperatures over the last 120 years.

areas where the changing climate better suits them. Lower latitudes are likely to get hotter and drier and mid-latitudes wetter and stormier. All this change, coupled with extreme loss of available habitat due to human activities, is not going to do species richness and overall biodiversity any good.

SAQ 3.5
Briefly distinguish between the roles of CFCs in the thinning of the ozone layer and the greenhouse effect.

International efforts to reduce carbon dioxide emissions

Just as CFCs brought governments together to try to save the ozone layer, the anthropogenic increase in greenhouse gases has also led to international concern. In 1988 a scientific advisory body, the Intergovernmental Panel on Climate Change (IPCC), was formed to report on the global situation. Its reports resulted in the Climate Change Convention, signed at the Rio Earth Summit held in Rio de Janeiro, Brazil in 1992, which set targets (but not binding ones) for the reduction of greenhouse gas emissions back to 1990 levels by the year 2000.

The 1997 Kyoto Protocol continued the efforts started in Rio, but recognised that the ideals of cutting emissions back to 1990 levels by 2000 were not going to be achieved. It targeted several greenhouse gases – CO_2, methane, nitrous oxide, various fluorocarbons and sulphur hexafluoride – and aimed to cut emissions to at least 5% below 1990 levels by 2012. These are more binding agreements than before and each nation has a specific target. For instance Japan must cut emissions by 6%, US by 7% and the European Union by 8% while Russia and New Zealand only have to keep to 1990 levels, and some countries, like Australia and Iceland, are allowed to increase emissions by up to 10%. The Kyoto Protocol allowed countries to trade in carbon emissions so that a country with fewer carbon emissions could 'sell' its quota to a rich over-producing country. Not everyone thinks this is a good arrangement as it lets some over-producers off the hook.

The climate change targets for greenhouse gases have been nothing like as successful as the Montreal Protocol for CFCs. This is probably due to a number of reasons. Firstly the destruction of the ozone layer was an evident fact, while the likelihood and consequences of global warming are still uncertain. Secondly, the technology existed to replace CFCs with less damaging products, but the developed world is so reliant on fossil fuels that they cannot be replaced easily with alternative energy sources. For developing countries, fossil fuels, especially coal, are abundant and relatively easy to exploit so it is likely that fossil fuel use will continue to increase in such countries. At the moment the developing countries contain about 80% of the world's people, but only consume 35% of the energy. This means it is up to the developed countries to make the major contribution to cutting greenhouse gas emissions.

Thirdly, it is possible that the targets are simply not attainable in our current political climate. It has been estimated that if no measures are taken to cut US emissions then they will *rise* by 34% by 2010! So to obtain a *fall* of 7% will be very difficult unless US domestic policy changes. In the long run, even stabilising atmospheric CO_2 at 560 ppm (twice the natural level) may require a reduction in emissions to 60% below 1990 levels! If the targets seem impossible to reach, then the major energy-consuming countries of the world may simply abandon any attempts to control greenhouse gases.

A number of approaches to reducing emissions have been suggested:
- Less reliance on fossil fuels and more on renewable ones such as solar power, wind power or nuclear energy. France reduced its carbon dioxide emissions during the 1980s by shifting electricity generation away from fossil fuels towards nuclear power.
- More energy-saving measures: the potential of this approach is underestimated and few in the consumer-driven countries of the US, Western Europe and Japan are really committed to energy saving. If Britain's houses were insulated like their Scandinavian counterparts, domestic heating bills would fall by a third.
- A lowering of expectation about standards of living. Almost every piece of technology we buy, including cars and televisions, requires large amounts of energy for its manufacture and use.

- The planting of more trees, allowing carbon dioxide to be locked away in wood.
- The development of alternatives to petrol and diesel to fuel cars, lorries and trains. We desperately need alternative, clean sources of energy. Scientists are currently developing a car run on hydrogen.
- More speculative solutions proposed include pumping carbon dioxide underground or down to the ocean floor, and even encouraging massive oceanic algal blooms to trap carbon dioxide in their organic matter.

What is needed is political willpower. Carbon dioxide emissions *can* be cut. Britain's peaked in 1973, just before the 1974 oil crisis, when they were equivalent to 178 million tonnes of carbon a year. In 1992 they were 156 million tonnes.

Energy consumption in the UK is still high and most of our energy comes from fossil fuels. Electricity generation is particularly wasteful as electricity is usually produced from fossil fuels and then turned into heat and light in the home. (Every time energy is transformed from one form to another some energy is lost, so the more conversion processes there are the more energy is wasted.) All these fuels produce CO_2 and other harmful gases (e.g. sulphur dioxide). But is there an environmentally friendly fuel?

In theory, wood burning is ecologically sound. Although burning releases CO_2, the wood is a **renewable resource** not a fossil fuel. However, where the demand for wood exceeds the capacity of forests to regenerate, serious deforestation can result. With the human population still growing (*figure 1.4* on page 5) and requiring ever more land on which to live and grow food, we simply do not have enough space for both people and forests for the renewable cropping of wood to be sustainable on a global basis.

Nuclear power does not release CO_2, but after the large radiation leak from the Chernobyl reactor in the Ukraine in 1986 it is not so popular. Decommissioning nuclear power stations and the storage of spent radioactive fuel are further problems. Water movements can be harnessed to generate electricity. However, water power from waves and hydroelectric dams in rivers may damage or disfigure coastal and river valley habitats. Solar panels are a bit unpredictable in the UK weather and are expensive in both materials and energy.

A final possibility is to harness the movement of air. Wind power is relatively inexpensive, but some people think modern wind farms are unsightly in the countryside (*figure 3.14*). They can be noisy, but new designs are quieter and they do seem to be one of the best ways to obtain clean energy. When (if ever) we develop new non-polluting sources of energy, we could always take the windmills down and would still have the countryside. The alternative may be not to have the wind farms, but at the risk of not having the natural countryside either.

● **Figure 3.14** A wind farm on Anglesey, North Wales.

SUMMARY

- Eutrophication occurs when excess nitrates, phosphates or organic matter get into the water system. It can lead to a loss of biodiversity.

- Biochemical (biological) oxygen demand can be used to assess the extent of eutrophication.

- Indicator species, such as lichens on land and invertebrate families in freshwater systems, can be used to assess pollution levels.

- Pesticides such as herbicides, fungicides and insecticides have helped to raise farm yields. However, they can cause very considerable damage to the wildlife of an area.

- One problem with DDT and PCBs is that their high fat solubility leads to them being concentrated up food chains.

- Heavy metal pollution is worst in areas where mining and smelting take place.

- Acid rain results from the presence of nitrogen oxides and sulphur oxides in the atmosphere and leads to damage to both terrestrial and aquatic ecosystems.

- Stratospheric levels of ozone have decreased sharply over the last 20 years as a result of halocarbons such as CFCs.

- The 1987 Montreal Protocol has greatly helped to reduce the damage to the ozone layer.

- Atmospheric carbon dioxide levels have risen steadily for some 200 years and seem likely to continue to do so.

- Raised levels of carbon dioxide, methane and certain other greenhouse gases are probably responsible for global warming.

- The consequences of global warming are still unclear but could be extremely serious for humans and other species alike.

- At the Rio Earth Summit in 1992 and in the Kyoto Protocol of 1997, many countries agreed to reduce their emissions of greenhouse gases.

Questions

1 Discuss the possible causes of eutrophication and explain how its consequences for the environment can be measured.

2 Discuss the dangers of cumulative poisons such as DDT and PCBs.

3 Describe the causes and consequences of acid rain. Suggest why its effects are so hard to reverse.

4 Discuss why, despite various international conventions, the holes in the ozone layer continue to grow and atmospheric levels of carbon dioxide continue to rise.

CHAPTER 4

Conservation of resources

By the end of this chapter you should be able to:

1 distinguish between *conservation* and *preservation*;

2 explain the different uses of the term *conservation*;

3 discuss economic and ethical reasons for conservation and the maintenance of biodiversity;

4 explain the need for conservation of fish populations in marine ecosystems;

5 describe measures that attempt to conserve fish stocks;

6 discuss how coal waste and china clay tips can be reclaimed;

7 explain the biological principles in the treatment of water for drinking;

8 discuss measures to reduce household waste and recycle useful commodities such as paper, glass and plastic bottles.

The meaning of conservation

Conservation and preservation

Conservation refers to the attempts by humans to preserve organisms and environments that are at risk as a result of human activity. But successful conservation requires a knowledge of ecology: how ecosystems function and how individual species fit into ecosystems. At its simplest, conservation involves the **preservation** of endangered habitats or species. Such preservation may entail the setting up of nature reserves or the establishment of captive breeding programmes.

Often, though, conservation requires the **management** of ecosystems. Grassland, for example, usually has to be managed in some way, otherwise succession occurs and the grassland becomes invaded by bushes and trees. This makes sense if you remember from page 10 that grassland is the result of a deflected succession. Grazing, mowing or occasional burning can help maintain grassland.

A still more active form of conservation occurs when damaged habitats are restored, a process known as **reclamation**. Eroded sand dunes, for instance, may be reclaimed by the erection of sea defences or by the planting of appropriate grasses that trap blown sand, allowing it to accumulate.

The most active form of conservation involves the **creation** of new habitats. At its simplest this may be nothing more than the digging of a new pond or the planting of a new hedge. A more ambitious scheme is currently under way in Derbyshire, Leicestershire and Staffordshire. Here a new National Forest is slowly being planted. It should eventually cover over 450 square kilometres and include some 30 million trees, most of them broad-leaved.

Creating habitats can be a very positive move in conservation, increasing the general diversity for wildlife, especially in areas already degraded by human activity. However, there is a risk that some planners and construction companies will argue that they can destroy important biological site A to put in their estate or road where it suits them because the habitat/ecosystem can be created anew at site B. This is, of course, a simplistic argument. The ecosystem occupies site A and not site B for a number of historical and environmental reasons. Trying to recreate a suitable habitat at B may be impossible, but that may only be realised after site A has been destroyed. So creating habitats may be ideal if they are additional sites for wildlife, but not as a substitute for the real thing. Which would you rather have, an original Leonardo da Vinci or a copy?

The relative importance of these four conservation activities – preservation, management, reclamation and creation – varies from country to country. A few countries still have a high proportion of their land covered with largely undamaged vegetation, supporting an abundance of native species. In such countries, preservation may be most important. In many countries, including Britain, human influence has been extensive and conservation may consist mainly of habitat management, reclamation and creation.

Conservation is dynamic in the sense that it is rarely sufficient simply to preserve – to surround a protected area with a fence and sit back. Conservationists have to be vigilant, keeping a lookout for political and other developments, and pro-active, anticipating changes in land use. Above all, successful conservation involves reconciling conflicts between the interests of local people, governments, industry, property developers, tourists and the wildlife itself.

The importance of conservation

Why bother to conserve and maintain biodiversity? Why not just let things take their course? Fundamentally there are two reasons: for the benefit of humans and for the benefit of other species.

Conservation for the benefit of humans can, to a certain extent, be described as the *economic* reason for conservation. This would include conservation of resources valuable to humans such as food plants and animals, organisms which may be a source of important genetic material, medicinal plants or even just conservation for pleasure (*figure 4.1*). Conservation for the benefit of other species can be described as the *ethical* reason for conservation: the conservation of species or ecosystems because they are there and have a right to remain so.

● **Figure 4.1** A family enjoying a walk in the Derbyshire Peak District.

When these two reasons come into conflict, humans generally win. Few people regret the worldwide extinction of the smallpox virus, or would regret the extinction of the mosquitoes that carry the malaria parasites. What is tragic is that many extinctions of species benefit only a few people for a short time. For instance, the destruction of the tropical rainforests is resulting in the extinction of many species: a loss of **biodiversity**. The gains are often short-lived and benefit few people – and rarely those who live in the forests. However, the long-term benefits from the preservation of tropical rainforest biodiversity are potentially huge.

Fisheries

The need to conserve fish stocks

Fish populations behave like any others – a population increases due to offspring produced by mature adult fish and immigration from other populations and decreases due to death (including fishing) and emigration. As far as the fishing industry is concerned, the important changes are the number of offspring that survive to join the population as juveniles (recruitment) and the deaths (including fishing catches).

Because we cannot tell at a glance what is going on in the vast oceans it is easy to ignore the possible effects of human activities. For centuries humans have used the oceans as a 'bottomless resource', dumping in everything from raw sewage to nuclear waste and unwanted bombs, and extracting fish with ever-increasing efficiency. The technology of trawler design has improved, including the development of huge drift nets and efficient bottom-dredging trawl nets. The use of sonar to detect shoals of fish, even from great distances, has tipped the balance: the hunters, fishermen, have become just too efficient as predators.

As early as 1890 fishermen noticed a drop in the quality of plaice caught in the North Sea, followed by haddock and cod by the 1920s. Next followed great reductions in the numbers of sardines in the Pacific by 1948, and in the Mediterranean by 1970. In 1992, the Canadian fishing industry collapsed; 40 000 jobs were lost and fish stocks are only recovering slowly. The United Nations Food and Agriculture Organisation (FAO) thinks that 60% of the oceans' fish stocks are being overfished with more fish being taken than can be replaced by recruitment. Even if fishing stopped completely, they estimate it would take 20 years for stocks to recover.

Oddly enough, one of the symptoms of unbalanced marine ecosystems looked initially like a success. Without the large populations of fish to eat them, sand-eels became much more abundant. Many seabirds also feed on sand-eels and they started to breed very successfully, so that species such as puffins thrived. The abundance of sand-eels was not missed by the beleaguered commercial fisheries, some of which switched to these small fish and literally began to vacuum them out of the sea in their millions for use in fertiliser and animal food. As you can imagine, the effect on the breeding of the puffins was not good.

Cod in the North Sea have been caught and sold when two years old. Yet cod does not reach adult maturity until it is four years old. So fewer young make it to mature breeding adults capable of replenishing population numbers. A far smaller percentage of the total young born reach adulthood than used to be the case, while the average size of fish now caught is much smaller than 50 years ago.

Solutions

Scientists from bodies such as the International Council for the Exploration of the Seas have tried to model fish populations and so produce an idea of the maximum sustainable yield for each species. These figures are transformed into fishing quotas for each country. In the European Union the Common Fisheries Policy, started in 1972 and finalised in 1983, sets total allowable catches for each country. The quotas are maintained in various ways including setting minimum mesh sizes for nets to regulate the sizes of fish caught and landed, by banning fishing in particular areas during breeding times for fish, licensing boats and by either decommissioning boats to decrease the size of the fleets, or restricting the time each vessel can be out fishing.

However, this regulation does not seem to be working. Possibly the understanding of fish biology (especially recruitment) and the models are faulty, so that predictions of sustainable yields are too high. For example, weather seems to make a big difference to the reproduction and survival of offspring in the Atlantic. There is worrying evidence that an increase in sea temperature, due to global warming, may be causing increased mortality in the very young fish. The quotas set may be over-optimistic. Certainly governments caught between a scientific report and real fishermen protesting for their livelihoods are likely to give the fishermen the largest quota they dare: no-one wants to tell fishermen their jobs have gone. Biologists may not have transmitted the urgency and importance of not over-fishing to governments and fisheries. Lastly, the fisheries may not be keeping to the quotas. It is impossible to adequately police fishing fleets to see that quotas are observed. Involving fishermen in data collection and quota management has helped considerably in some areas. Trust and co-operation between scientists, governments and fishermen are needed to make fish stocks safe.

Another problem is **bycatch**, that is the animals that are caught in the nets and subsequently returned to the sea as unwanted, because they are damaged, immature or the wrong species. About 25% of the world catch is discarded in this way. Most animals thrown back have little chance of survival as many of them are dead, injured or in shock and many predators (seagulls and sharks alike) know to follow fishing vessels for an easy

● **Figure 4.2** Cages containing farmed salmon in the Western Isles of Scotland.

meal. Fishermen with a quota are likely to try to optimise their profit from the catch by discarding all but the most profitable fish and thereby increasing their bycatch. Better fishing nets, designed to catch only large fish, should help to reduce bycatch by allowing small fish and juveniles to escape undamaged. A phasing out of high seas drift nets from 2002 will also help conserve fish.

Fish stocks all over the world have suffered from overfishing and with the world human population rising there will be extra demand for fish in the future. The long-lasting solution may be fish farming or **aquaculture** (*figure 4.2*). About 15–20% of fish and shellfish come from aquaculture, with China contributing 60% to this total, and many hope this will rise in order to take the pressure off wild stocks. However nothing is achieved without a price. Fish farming requires high levels of pesticides and antibiotics to be used. It pollutes large amounts of water, causes eutrophication, intensifies fish disease, and may lead to the escape of genetically different fish into wild populations or the introduction of new fish species into an area, which could disrupt the ecosystem. In some parts of the world, it also results in the destruction of mangrove swamps.

*SAQ 4.1*_____

State four measures that can help preserve wild fish stocks.

Land reclamation

Industrial waste

Many industrial and manufacturing sites are associated with **urban areas** and about 80% of the people in the UK live in urban areas. Urban areas contain a number of habitats that are suitable for wildlife: gardens, verges, railway embankments, canals, sewage treatment plants, parks, golf courses, churchyards, cemeteries and vacant or derelict land. Derelict areas within this urban setting can be upgraded to form wildlife havens (*figure 4.3*) and these places make excellent havens for humans, too.

The UK is a highly industrialised country and decades of high levels of mining, energy production, iron-ore smelting, chemical manufacture and other industrial production have left much contaminated and damaged land. Toxic wastes not only threaten the health of humans living or playing in the area, but also damage or destroy natural wildlife. The waste products of industry are often dumped as slag heaps, which are unsightly and take decades to blend into the landscape. Many tips created by mining are contaminated with heavy metals in concentrations that are toxic to most plants (see page 30). Mining, of course, occurs anywhere the minerals are found, often in beautiful countryside and National Parks (*figure 3.5* on page 31). Here we will look at two particular types of mining waste: coal tips, which are the most widespread industrial waste; and china clay tips, which are a more restricted and unusual waste found in southwest England.

Coal waste

Both open cast mining (surface quarrying) and deep shaft mining of coal seams create colliery waste or spoil heaps. These are a common feature in the coal-producing areas of south Wales, central and northern England and central Scotland. Although very little coal is now mined in the UK, the results of over a century of coal extraction have left many vast spoil heaps. The waste is usually a mixture of shale, clay, sand, coal fragments and various iron compounds. They are not only unsightly, but are also a source of contaminated

● **Figure 4.3** The Jupiter Urban Wildlife Project was started in 1990 to transform disused railway sidings in industrial Grangemouth, Scotland, into a wildlife garden.   **a** The site before landscaping in July 1991. **b** A view of the main pond after landscaping.

water due to run-off and may even spontaneously combust under certain circumstances!

Coal waste does not readily support vegetation. This is partly because the slopes of the tips are often steep and compacted so water runs off the surfaces. Tips from the north of England coal fields also have a high iron pyrite (FeS_2) content because of the boggy anoxic conditions in which the Carboniferous swamp vegetation, now fossilised to form the coal, once grew. The pyrite oxidises on contact with air and makes the tip very acidic at the surface. Tips weather slowly, so nutrients like nitrogen and phosphorus are not released for plants to use.

Left to itself, mining spoil slowly turns into heathland with heather and grasses tolerant of

acidic conditions. One such open cast tip, Seckar Lane near Wakefield in Yorkshire, was abandoned in 1950. It contained wet areas that are now full of orchids and bogmoss and is so interesting it was made an SSSI (see pages 54–55) in 1984. Many old coal tips were left to recolonise slowly and naturally and are now interesting sites for wildlife. The low nutrient content of the tips ensures that a diversity of species is present, including lichens, mosses and fungi, none of which compete well with rampant vegetation in nutrient-rich sites. The quality of vegetation seems related to pH: the lower the pH the fewer the species found.

Regeneration can be speeded up somewhat if the tip is landscaped to remove steep slopes and seeded (without any fertiliser added) with a suitable grass mix. Indeed, contouring to remove dangerously steep slopes, which could otherwise cause landslides, is always to be recommended whatever the extent of reclamation thereafter. Liming with crushed limestone worked into the surface of the tip to neutralise the acidity of the pyrite will also accelerate regeneration.

Unfortunately perhaps for wildlife, in the speed of society today many people are too impatient to wait for natural regeneration, and when you see the vast depressing expanses of colliery spoil you can see why. Grand landscaping designs get drawn up with massive soil-moving, acid-neutralising, fertilising, seeding, tree-planting and turfing projects. Such schemes, although well meant, do often run into trouble. Creating designer habitats from reclaimed land is difficult, time consuming and expensive. If non-native seed mixes are used, unwanted plant species may be introduced; planted trees often need aftercare to prevent their death and some plant communities specified by the landscape designers may just not have the right conditions to establish.

Many tips are out in the countryside and are best just returned to a natural vegetation to blend

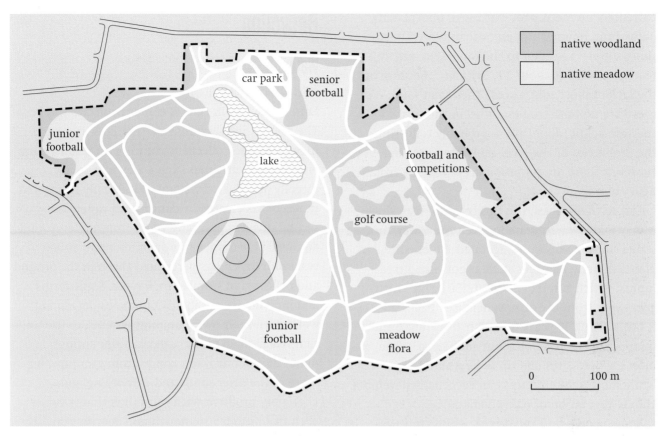

● **Figure 4.4** Plan of Central Forest Park in Stoke-on-Trent, UK, which was constructed on derelict colliery spoil tips between 1969 and 1974.

in with their surroundings. Those allowed to regenerate naturally are the best for wildlife, but others have been successfully turned into cultivatable farmland. Some, closest to urban areas, have been transformed into amenities – parks and recreation grounds. *Figure 4.4* shows the plan of an urban park in Stoke-on-Trent. This land was once derelict colliery spoil, but is now a park with areas for games and sport as well as a lake, meadows and woods.

China clay

White, conical china clay spoil tips are a typical sight in parts of Devon and Cornwall where mining for china clay started in about 1770. The fine china clay, also called kaolinite, is used in paper-making and, as its name suggests, for making china. The deposits of clay are deep but they contain about six times as much sand as clay, so the dug clay has to be cleaned and the sand is dumped in large heaps (*figure 4.5*).

About 5 million tonnes of sand a year are produced. These mounds are about 97% sand

(grains of quartz). They are a hostile environment for colonisation by plants. To start with, the slopes are so steep and the sand so pure, with only 1–2% silt or clay, that they are unstable. Rain quickly drains through the sand and leaches out any remaining soluble nutrients so the sand tips are

● **Figure 4.5** White sand tips produced during china clay mining north of St Austell, Cornwall. Notice the unstable white slopes and heathland vegetation.

extremely nutrient poor. Nitrogen, phosphorus, potassium, magnesium and calcium are all in short supply: nitrogen in the top 20 cm only reaches a level of about 10–30 kg ha^{-1}. Because of the lack of most substances other than sand, there are no buffering qualities in the tips, so they are acidic, about pH 4, probably reflecting the properties of the local rainwater (see page 31). However, there are no problems of toxicity from heavy metals.

Left to themselves, the tips colonise very slowly. It may take over 20 years for even the lower, more stable slopes to become vegetated. Colonising plants include legumes such as gorse and tree lupins, which can fix about 50–150 kg ha^{-1} nitrogen a year from the atmosphere (see pages 20–21). It takes about 50 years for soil nitrogen to build up to a normal level of about 1000 kg ha^{-1}. The most exposed sites end up as heathland (*figure 4.5*) while more sheltered tips can eventually develop a climax vegetation of oak woodland.

Some people find the bright, white sand pyramids a distinctive feature of the landscape, akin to massive works of art, but for many they are an eyesore. To speed up colonisation and ensure they quickly blend into the countryside, the slopes are contoured to lessen their steepness and make the mounds more stable and then they are sprayed with seed mixed with wet wood pulp or peat. Better yet is to cover the contoured slopes with soil, wherever possible taken locally from work sites such as road-widening schemes. Young trees can then be planted and the bare soil seeded with a mix of grasses and legumes (clover and bird'sfoot trefoil). To maintain vegetation in soil with such poor nutrient quality, additional nitrogen-rich fertiliser has to be added as aftercare for many years.

SAQ 4.2

List five reasons why the natural colonisation of china clay mounds is so slow.

Recycling

Water

Water extraction for drinking

Drinking water in the UK comes from two sources. The first is directly from rain that falls in a catchment area and collects by running off into streams and rivers. Sometimes such water is pumped directly out of river systems, but usually it is stored in reservoirs created by damming a valley. The second involves pumping water from underground aquifers. This is ancient rainwater, up to 10 000 years old, which has percolated through the ground and collected in suitable rock types. Some farms and individual households tap the underground water with their own pumping systems, or use wells that reach down to the water table or springs. About 35% of our water comes from groundwater, more in the drier south and east of England.

The big problem with rainfall is that it varies both from month to month and year to year. This means the flow of water in rivers is also variable (*figure 4.6*). Unfortunately for water companies, the hot summer droughts coincide with the highest demand for water for irrigating crops and watering gardens. As is indicated in *figure 4.6*, drought has been more of a problem in recent years. Surface water supplies can become scarce very

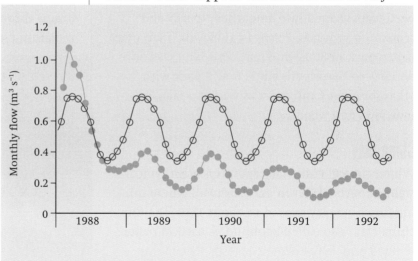

● **Figure 4.6** Actual monthly flow rates for the period 1988–92 (orange dots) for the river Babingley, a small chalk stream in Norfolk, UK. The open blue circles show the average flow rates for 1976–88 superimposed on each year so direct comparison can be made between the average and recent years. Notice how low the flow rates were between 1989 and 1992.

rapidly, and water-conserving methods, such as domestic hosepipe bans, have to be introduced during very dry summers. Care is needed to leave sufficient water in the river system for it to function properly. It might be thought that aquifers, with their vast underground reservoirs, are an ideal solution but they too are not being replenished and in some years the water table falls substantially so that wetland habitats and their wildlife come under threat.

Supplying a large city with clean water fit for drinking can pose quite a problem. In the nineteenth century, the rapidly growing cities of the industrial north, such as Manchester, Leeds and Bradford, used the clean catchment areas of the Pennines to collect water. This was left to settle in reservoirs, to remove suspended particles and reduce pathogenic organisms, before being filtered and disinfected. Nowadays, catchments are rarely unpolluted and reservoirs empty more rapidly because of increasing demand, so more reliance has to be put on subsequent filtering and chemical treatment. However, it is still easiest (and cheapest) to collect and store water in upland catchment areas – which also tend to have a high annual rainfall. Water for drinking is usually first filtered in a sand tank, or rotating microstrainer drum, to remove the algae which can make the water taste mouldy. Further, slower, filtering removes finer particles and organic impurities.

Both pesticides and fertilisers are so widely used that both occur in our drinking water and cost water companies a considerable amount to control. Nitrates in tap water often exceed recommended levels in areas that have intensive farming. These areas are called Nitrate Sensitive Areas (NSAs), where nitrates are close to, or exceed, the European Community Drinking Water Directive of $50\,mg\,dm^{-3}$. Farmers in such areas have been encouraged to reduce nitrate run-off by converting arable to grass and reducing nitrogen applications. Although to be phased out in 2003, NSAs are now included in Nitrate Vulnerable Zones where nitrate control is obligatory (see page 60). Nitrates can be removed by ion exchange or biological denitrification using heterotrophs that take oxygen from the nitrate and release nitrogen. Aluminium or iron salts may be added to cause suspended

particles to flocculate (clump together) so they can be filtered out. Chlorine or ozone is added to kill microorganisms; any excess chlorine is then removed using sulphur dioxide. If any traces of organic pollutants remain they can be filtered out using activated carbon filters. Finally, fluoride may be added which can reduce dental cavities in those who drink it regularly.

A particular pollution problem is the occurrence of the protozoan *Cryptosporidium*, which can get into catchment water from nearby slurry lagoons, grazing land or fields treated by muck spreading. In 1993, 400 000 people became ill in Wisconsin, US, after water was contaminated with farm waste containing *Cryptosporidium*. The oocysts can survive for years and are very hard to kill without adding so much chlorine that the water tastes bad. Minimising contamination risks and efficient filtering are the best ways of dealing with this problem. Cyanobacterial blooms can be a hazard in reservoirs in summer as they release toxins into the water and can make it taste unpleasant, while in peaty catchment areas the organic content of the peat can turn the water an unappetising deep brown, especially during the first heavy rains after a drought or a moorland fire.

Water from underground aquifers is often cleaner than surface water. Sometimes it just needs oxidation to remove iron and manganese salts (which can then be removed by filtering), and carbon dioxide (which is not dangerous to humans, but tends to corrode the machinery). Any biological contamination can then be removed by the usual disinfectant treatment. However, aquifers too can become polluted from leaking sewage systems, drainage from landfill sites, percolation of agricultural and industrial chemicals into the groundwater and contamination from mines. A badly polluted aquifer may take hundreds or even thousands of years to return to normal.

Sewage disposal

Having taken so much care extracting and treating water for human use, we end up with human waste products that must also be treated before they are released back into the aquatic system (rivers or sea) if they are not to cause serious pollution problems.

In Britain we do not separate human excrement waste from less damaging wastes such as bathwater, so the sewage that reaches treatment plants is very dilute. After a coarse filter removes large items such as cloth and animal corpses, a macerator breaks up the sewage. At this point it has a BOD (see page 26) of around $600\,mg\,O_2\,dm^{-3}\,5\,day^{-1}$. The sewage is allowed to settle in tanks, where its BOD decreases by 30–40%; the liquid is filtered off and colonies of bacteria and protozoa are added. In old sewage works, the liquid is run along slowly rotating pipes over large round filter beds, which are filled with crushed rock covered in bacteria. These are called trickling filter beds. The rotating pipes are often attended by a flock of starlings that hop over each arm as it reaches them. The BOD of the water flowing from the filter bed is about $60\,mg\,O_2\,dm^{-3}\,5\,day^{-1}$. After a second settling process the water BOD falls to $20\,mg\,O_2\,dm^{-3}\,5\,day^{-1}$ and is clean enough to be released into the river system.

An alternative system, the activated sludge process, uses large tanks to aerate the liquid from settling tanks, to which bacteria and protozoa are added to decompose the organic matter. The resulting fluid settles in large ponds until the liquid is clear enough to be released into the river. The sludge has to be treated further. Even cleaned-up sewage may still contain viruses and bacteria harmful to humans, such as poliomyelitis or infectious hepatitis.

Household waste

Most of us throw all our household waste into a bag or bin to be collected once a week by the local refuse department. We probably never think of it again, but of course it has to be taken somewhere and most councils simply dump it in pits in open field sites. These rubbish tips are smelly and attract rats, flies and noisy birds such as crows and gulls. Once a site is full it has to be sealed and landscaped, but it is unsuitable for many uses because of subsidence as the rubbish rots and settles. It also emits methane, which is bad news as it is a greenhouse gas (see page 37). In some farsighted schemes the landfill sites are designed so the methane can be collected and used as fuel. If all the methane produced on rubbish sites in

Britain was collected it could provide the energy equivalent of about two million tonnes of coal!

About 20% of household waste is sent to special incinerators where it is burned to produce useful energy directly. In Sheffield, 3500 homes are heated by a council incinerator that burns rubbish. Converting waste into heat or electrical energy, rather than dumping it in landfill sites, seems like an excellent idea, but some environmental groups, including Friends of the Earth, oppose incineration because of the risks of pollution.

Most of our rubbish is not really rubbish: it doesn't have to be thrown away. The keyword is **recycling**, and if everyone took care to recycle what they could, the tremendous pressure on landfill sites could be eased. Recycling materials that would otherwise be thrown away includes **re-using** items in their original form or sending them to a factory to be pulped or melted down and re-formed into useful articles. Recycling products like plastic, paper and textiles *saves* 3–6 times the energy that would be obtained by incinerating them. This is because it takes much less energy to recycle a product than to create it from raw materials such as wood, oil, unspun cotton and so on. In many cases recycling also creates less pollution than making new products.

Recycling takes a bit of effort but is something everyone can do. Many city and county councils now produce leaflets stating their environmental policies on issues such as pollution, water resources, transport and recycling. A few UK councils provide door-to-door collections for recyclable material (*figure 4.7*). Many more have collection points at convenient places (often car parks and supermarkets) where items such as bottles, paper, books, cans, some plastics, aluminium foil and textiles can be left by members of the public. They may also run extra services such as Christmas tree shredding and a collection service for old refrigerators so that the ozone-damaging CFC coolants can be removed safely.

Recycling can save both the natural resources of the Earth and the energy used to manufacture new products. For example, one tonne of paper requires wood pulp from about 16 trees. Recycling paper therefore saves trees. Glass recycling avoids quarrying for silica. Making an aluminium can from recycled material uses 20 times less energy than making a can from raw materials, as well as saving the natural environment in areas of the world where aluminium ore is mined. Kitchen waste can largely be recycled by composting it and using it in the garden. Any material that is recycled or composted instead of thrown away decreases the volume of rubbish which otherwise goes into landfill sites. The UK government set a target that, by the year 2000, 25% of all waste had to be recycled. However, in 1995 only about 5% of waste was recycled and it seems unlikely that the 25% target will be met even by 2005 without more encouragement. In Germany, over 30% recycling is achieved by a complex system of coloured bags and boxes, including a black bag for non-recyclable rubbish destined for landfill which householders have to pay to have removed. This has cut down the waste considerably!

Re-using items in their original form is even better than re-making things because it saves even the energy needed to reprocess the recycled materials. Often there are other benefits. Charities can raise money by selling donated clothing and other items and send clothing and blankets to benefit people in disaster areas.

Many things can be re-used:

- returnable bottles (milk and some soft drinks);
- jars and bottles (which can be passed on to marmalade and wine makers);
- paper only used on one side, envelopes, cards and calendars (which can be used for gift tags or children's art classes);
- clothes in good condition (which can be used by charities);
- plastic carrier bags.

We all **consume** a great deal in a year: food, water, washing materials, clothes, and energy in the form of heat, light and fuel. You can add to the list yourself. What we buy and how we use it can have an influence on the energy and materials consumed in production, the amount of pollution caused during production and use, and the waste created in discarding the product. We can ask many questions as we make choices about our consumerism:

● **Figure 4.7** An electric collection cart being used for the door-to-door recycling scheme in Haringey, London. The green box carries the recycling symbol.

- Is the packaging of this article wasteful – can I buy a refill pack?
- Does this wood come from a renewable plantation or from a tropical forest?
- Does this aerosol emit CFCs?
- Is there an alternative to slug pellets?
- Is this vegetable genetically engineered and if so is it more or less harmful to the environment than an unmodified one?
- Can I find an alternative to bog peat for the garden? (Coconut fibre and cocoa seedcases are renewable resources; shredded treefern trunks are not!)
- Is this cotton or paper unbleached?
- Has this food been grown using a minimum of environmentally damaging pesticides?
- Which of these cans of tuna is dolphin friendly?
- Have I left a light or radiator on needlessly?
- Is this paper recycled?

SAQ 4.3

Distinguish between re-using and recycling.

SAQ 4.4

Is the repeated use of milk bottles an instance of re-use?

SUMMARY

◆ Conservation refers to attempts by humans to preserve organisms and environments that are at risk as a result of human activity.

◆ Conservation may entail preservation, management, reclamation or habitat creation.

◆ Conservation is dynamic in that the passive protection of an area is rarely sufficient.

◆ Conservation can be economically advantageous.

◆ There are ethical reasons why we should conserve nature.

◆ Although various practices, including the imposition of quotas, are of value, wild fish stocks continue to be over-fished.

◆ Land rendered derelict by industrial activity can be reclaimed for use.

◆ Coal waste and china clay tips present different ecological problems.

◆ Water purification relies on a combination of physical, chemical and biological processes.

◆ Attempts are being made to reduce the amount of household waste that is simply dumped in landfill sites.

◆ The re-use and recycling of products can help conserve resources.

Questions

1 Explain what is meant by conservation and discuss the arguments in favour of conservation.

2 How can fish stocks be conserved? Suggest why fish conservation has few if any 'success stories'.

3 Suppose that you are an applied ecologist. Describe the similarities and differences posed by the reclamation of coal waste and china clay tips.

4 Explain the principles behind purification of water for drinking.

CHAPTER 5

National conservation issues

By the end of this chapter you should be able to:

1 explain how ecologically important areas are protected in the UK with particular reference to National Parks, Sites of Special Scientific Interest (SSSIs) and Environmentally Sensitive Areas (ESAs);

2 describe the major conservation issues facing the management of National Parks;

3 explain the role of the Royal Society for the Protection of Birds (RSPB) in protecting ecologically important areas in the UK;

4 discuss the significance of voluntary conservation bodies in the UK.

Conservation in the UK

An impoverished situation

Compared to many countries, the UK is poor in natural, unspoiled habitats, although we do still have much diversity – woodlands, blanket and raised peat bogs, lowland heaths, salt marshes and chalk grassland, for example. Many habitats are important because of their long history: ancient coppiced woodland (*figure 5.1*) and water meadows have taken thousands of years to develop rich floras and faunas. If they are destroyed they can never be recreated in the same way; as when a favourite vase is smashed, even if it is glued together again the cracks will still be there. The extent of our ancient woodland has shrunk in area from 1650 kha in 1086 (the Domesday Book) through 600 kha in 1890 to just 300 kha in 2000.

Most of the British Isles countryside is farmland. Consider the Yorkshire Dales with their dry stone walls and fields dotted with barns (*figure 2.2* on page 11), the sheep-grazed downs of the south of England, the enormous fields and huge skies of East Anglia (*figure 2.1* on page 10), the rugged deer and grouse moors of Scotland and the rolling green fields of Northern Ireland. All these are the result of generations of human management, even if this influence is more obvious in some landscapes than in others. Overall, it is a rich landscape and we will do well to protect both the remaining patches of natural ecosystems and the historic farmed countryside with its associated wildlife. There is also the task of restoring

● **Figure 5.1** This ancient wood, Hayley Wood in Cambridgeshire, was being coppiced for poles and firewood 750 years ago. The tall trees are oak and ash; some hazel and ash have just been coppiced (cut down close to the ground) and will soon grow back.

and regenerating the degraded areas damaged by industrial use and intensive agricultural activity (see pages 14, 28 and 45).

Protected sites

Within the UK's historical, densely populated landscape it is important to be able to identify sites worth protecting. An important site might be small: a patch of rare orchids, a flood meadow that has never been drained, a raised bog, an ancient woodland with a thousand years of recorded history or a hay meadow never spoilt by fertiliser enrichment. Or it might be large: the chalk downs, northern upland blanket bog, the whole of the Lake District with its Ice Age-carved glacial features, a coastline of mudflats and estuaries or an offshore island.

In the US, large tracts of wilderness (Yellowstone and Yosemite National Parks, for example) are set aside entirely for wildlife and their human visitors. In the States these parks are owned by the Federal Government, whereas in the UK most land is privately owned and is already intensively used. So UK conservation measures have to take into account the reality that people make their living from the same areas that contain ecosystems that are worth conserving in their own right.

The protection of sites, to maintain their ecological value, is the main aim of a number of conservation bodies. In the UK, voluntary organisations play an important role, especially in protecting smaller sites such as those mentioned above. Government legislation tends to have most influence on the larger land areas of the National Parks and Environmentally Sensitive Areas. These are mainly designated for their attractive landscapes. In addition, though, there are legislative measures for small sites and even single trees. Small sites include National and Local Nature Reserves and Sites of Special Scientific Interest, which are oriented towards the conservation of species or habitats.

Although designated sites have **statutory protection** (i.e. protection in the eyes of the law) there are ways this can be legally bypassed, which gravely weakens the protection afforded to wildlife. Existing legislation falls into two categories. One is concerned with the preservation of important *habitats*; the other with the preservation of particular *species*. On page 42 we saw how conservation involves preservation, management, reclamation *and* habitat creation. Existing UK legislation addresses only one of these four areas: preservation – though management plans are often agreed upon with landowners.

The UK, in common with many other countries, has a large number of **conservation voluntary bodies**, also known as **non-governmental organisations** (**NGOs**). Such voluntary bodies direct the enthusiasm and talent of millions of people to conservation issues. In addition to obtaining and managing land for the benefit of nature, they also act as pressure groups helping to prevent further damage to the environment. Their income comes from membership subscriptions, company sponsorships, appeals, legacies and the sale of goods. They also often qualify for grants from local authorities or government sources.

Some voluntary bodies have aims wider than nature conservation. For instance, the **National Trust** (founded in 1895) also owns and conserves a large number of buildings. We shall look in detail at two charities that concentrate on nature conservation. One, the RSPB, was formed towards the end of the nineteenth century and devotes its efforts to a particular group of organisms; the other, the Woodland Trust, is a relatively new organisation and concentrates on a particular habitat.

SSSIs

Sites of Special Scientific Interest (**SSSIs**) are areas of particular scientific importance. Most are important for ecological reasons, but a significant number are geological SSSIs, with rich collections of fossils or particular rock formations. The formal definition of an SSSI is 'an area of land which is of

	SSSIs	NNRs
England	4063	200
Scotland	1448	71
Wales	973	62
Total	6484	333

● **Table 5.1** The number of Sites of Special Scientific Interest (SSSIs) and National Nature Reserves (NNRs) in 1999. NNRs are discussed on page 59.

special interest by reason of its flora, fauna, geological or physiographical features'. Ecological SSSIs are usually quite small but contain important habitats. They include ancient woodlands (Hayley Wood, *figure 5.1*, is an SSSI), rich areas of chalk grassland, lowland heaths, reservoirs with wetland birds, old clay and gravel pits and disused quarries, even the occasional open cast coal tip (as mentioned on page 46). As you can see from this list, many SSSI habitats are on sites created by human activity and subsequently occupied by interesting communities of plants and animals.

By 1999 there were a total of 6484 listed SSSIs in England, Scotland and Wales (*table 5.1*) and the number of sites is steadily rising. On average about 7% of the land in England is designated as SSSIs, but this varies from county to county – Cumbria has about 12%, while central England (counties like Bedfordshire, Northamptonshire and Cambridgeshire) has less than 3% of the area. There are even 26 SSSIs in London. Northern Ireland does not have SSSIs, having instead its own **Areas of Special Scientific Interest**. Depending on location, SSSIs are the responsibility of English Nature, Scottish Natural Heritage or the Countryside Council for Wales.

Category of damage	1990/91	1991/92	1992/93	1993/94	1994/95
Short-term – 'could recover, in less than 15 years, with favourable management'.	212	196	126	111	76
Long-term – 'lasting reduction of SSSI, or more than 15 years to recover'.	31	47	46	39	48
Partial loss – 'result in denotification of part of SSSI'.	10	6	7	11	14
Complete loss	0	1	0	0	0
Overall totals	253	250	179	161	154

● **Table 5.2** Damage to Sites of Special Scientific Interest (SSSIs) in England, Scotland and Wales between 1990 and 1995. In 1993 there were 6000 SSSIs. Note that the overall fall in total is due to falls in the short-term damage category only.

The important feature of SSSIs is that local planning authorities and landowners or occupiers must be informed of activities that might damage the site. In theory this should protect them from development as English Nature (or its equivalent in Scotland or Wales) have to be informed of any potential threat to the site and can negotiate better management to preserve its value. In practice, however, development for roads (*figure 5.2*), housing or leisure amenities all too often takes place. A number of SSSIs are damaged each year (*table 5.2*). Although the number does seem to have fallen in recent years, the number of SSSIs which are suffering from long-term damage or partial loss may even be rising. Some government money is available to help protect SSSIs, but almost no central funding exists to finance their management.

National Parks

The origin and function of National Parks

A **National Park** in England or Wales is an area of substantial size and outstandingly attractive scenery that is specially protected and reserved for public enjoyment. Other countries have had National Parks for over 100 years. The first ever National Park, Yellowstone Park in Wyoming, US, was established in 1872, followed by several more in the 1890s.

● **Figure 5.2** The M3 extension under construction in 1993. The road cut through an SSSI on Twyford Down, Hampshire.

However, none existed in the UK before 1949, heralded by the passing of the National Parks and Access to the Countryside Act. This Act went through the Houses of Parliament in a spirit of post-Second World War optimism and hope for the future.

A National Park was defined in 1945 as:

'an extensive area of beautiful and relatively wild country in which, for the nation's benefit and by appropriate national decision and action:

- the characteristic landscape beauty is strictly preserved;
- access and facilities for public open-air enjoyment are amply provided;
- wildlife and buildings and places of architectural and historical interest are suitably protected; while
- established farming use is effectively maintained'.

The first National Park was the Peak District (*figure 5.3*), soon followed by nine others (*figure 5.4*). The Norfolk and Suffolk Broads is now also considered a National Park, although under slightly different legislation. In the Broads the linked system of waterways, reed beds and fens are the result of long periods of peat-digging from the twelfth to the fourteenth century. They lie in an area of intensive crop production and are damaged by nitrates from farm runoff and by ploughing of the marshland for the planting of crops. Between them the National Parks have a total area of 14 055 km^2, 8% of the area of England and Wales.

The South Downs and New Forest may become National

● **Figure 5.3** Lathkilldale in the Peak District National Park, the first National Park in England or Wales. This dale is also a National Nature Reserve.

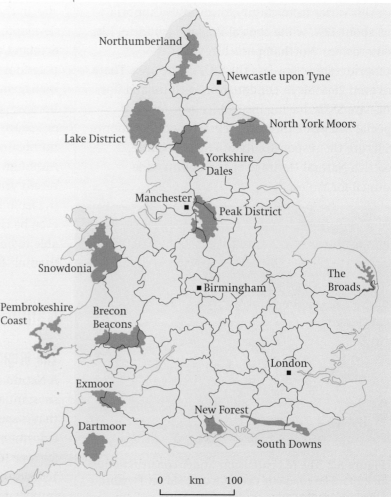

● **Figure 5.4** The National Parks of England and Wales. The New Forest and South Downs are shown in a different colour as they are not yet National Parks.

Parks, but the process of consultation and setting up takes several years. The South Downs are rich chalk grasslands first cleared in Neolithic times. Grazing by sheep and rabbits maintains this deflected succession and keeps the highly competitive grasses from outgrowing the lovely flowers for which the Downs are famous. The New Forest has a unique history as it was formed in 1079 by William I as a hunting park.

As you can see from their official description above, the main function of National Parks is not the conservation of natural ecosystems but the protection of recognised landscapes. Legislation permits farming, forestry and quarrying to take place in them. People live and work in the parks as well as use them for recreation, but any activity that might change the nature of the park, such as road building, housing or quarrying, needs planning permission.

Nine parks are centred on large areas of upland, which are more sparsely inhabited and less intensively farmed than lowland sites; they all have good access for those tourists who like walking on the hills. Many beautiful lowland areas are more intensively farmed and do not have free access for visitors, so have instead been designated **Areas of Outstanding Natural Beauty** (AONBs) (see page 60).

About 13% of land in the National Parks in England and Wales is also designated as SSSIs. Scotland and Northern Ireland do not have National Parks. Scotland has 40 **National Scenic Areas**, defined in 1978, which are more like AONBs. Northern Ireland has **Areas of Outstanding Natural Beauty** (with a different designation to the AONBs in England and Wales).

Major conservation issues in National Parks

Each National Park is a patchwork of habitats including farmland, woods, upland moors, towns and villages. Half the parks also have coastlines. Each park has its own specific management issues, which include woodland management schemes, informal agreements with landowners or tenant farmers, the protection of archaeological sites and the education of local communities. A priority for conservation is the identification, protection and management of important ecological sites. Some conservation problems are specific to particular parks. Large areas of Dartmoor, for example, are used by the military so the public are excluded. At the same time, there are several management problems to do with farming, mining and tourism that are common to most or all of the parks.

Farming methods

Back in 1949, the British landscape, considered so attractive, was the result of centuries of traditional farming methods. Even then, just after the Second World War, farming was beginning to change radically. The drive for self-sufficiency during the war heralded the intensification of agriculture (see pages 13–16).

Most National Parks in England are actually very similar in their agricultural systems, with large uplands grazed by sheep or managed for grouse shooting. The valleys tend to be hay meadows or fields for dairy cows and beef cattle (*figure 2.2* on page 11). Naturally, those who try to earn a living from the land wish to maximise their income especially when prices for farm produce are so low. Consequently, changes in livestock production are the biggest threat to the traditions of the parks. This happens, for example, when areas of moorland are ploughed up to improve grazing for animals. The Wildlife and Countryside Act of 1981 provided opportunities for management agreements with farmers and landowners to 'conserve or enhance the natural beauty or amenity of the land or promote its enjoyment by the public'. Included in this was the preservation of moorland.

In Scotland the expansion of forestry is the main threat to the National Scenic Areas. Scottish Natural Heritage monitors changes, but better protection of the scenic beauty and heritage occurs in areas owned by the National Trust for Scotland, a voluntary body that considers conservation uppermost in all proposals. Some very important habitats, such as bog woodland, were drained for tree planting. Recently the ecological value of these internationally rare habitats has been recognised and the Forestry Commission has started to fell parts of the plantations and restore the wetlands.

Parks in England where forestry has a major impact include the Northumberland and the North

York Moors National Parks. Each of these has about 20% of its area as non-native conifer plantations. By the 1970s there was considerable pressure on most National Parks from expanding forestry plantations. The ruthless planting of the post-war period has now changed to a more sympathetic approach to forestry. New planting is now more carefully planned to ensure appropriate tree species are planted, and only in areas where the forests will be less intrusive. Felling practices too are now designed to have less impact on the countryside.

Mining

In the Peak District National Park there are several small, family-run mines around Castleton. Here the rare and beautiful mineral Blue John is dug out and made into jewellery and other small items. The mines are open to tourists and the whole of Castleton seems to thrive on Blue John. However, at the other end of the village is a completely different mining operation – an open cast quarry where limestone is extracted. Mining for lead, millstone grit and limestone has been a constant threat to the beautiful scenery of the Peak District and quarrying companies still wish to expand operations.

Quarrying occurs in most National Parks: slate in Snowdonia; lead and limestone in the Yorkshire Dales; iron, alum and coal in the North York Moors; iron, tin and china clay in Dartmoor. Some mining spoil – lead and copper, for example – leaves the ground polluted with heavy metals (see pages 30 and 46 and *figure 3.5* on page 31). Extraction of millstone grit and limestone, although noisy and dusty, is less damaging in the long term. Left to regenerate, limestone quarries have the potential to become fantastic wildlife sites resembling natural cliffs and rock falls. Modern mining operations often have 'clear-up contracts' which usually include landscaping after the mining has finished but may over-tidy a potentially interesting site (see page 46).

Tourism

The very popularity of the UK's National Parks is a testament to their success and their value to the millions of people living in urban situations who want to 'get away from it all' at weekends and for

● **Figure 5.5** An eroded path being repaired in the Brecon Beacons, Powys.

holidays (*figure 4.1* on page 43). The Peak District, for example, lies at the heart of industrial England and is surrounded by the cities of Manchester, Huddersfield, Sheffield, Macclesfield, Derby and Stoke-on-Trent. The ever-increasing success of recreational areas leads to huge numbers of visitors and great strain on the roads, footpaths and amenities. Erosion of vegetation due to trampling is especially serious in upland and coastal sites, where the slow-growing native plants take a long time to recover from any damage (*figure 5.5*). The presence of too many tourists can also disturb the resident animals, especially mammals and birds during their breeding seasons.

To cope with so much traffic puts pressure on authorities to widen and upgrade small country roads, build new ones and install massive car parks. Even this does not alleviate Bank Holiday congestion. Radical schemes to ban tourist cars and provide public transport within some parks have been suggested.

The huge numbers of visitors can overload existing amenities of power supply and waste disposal. The Norfolk and Suffolk Broads have special problems associated with their heavy use by boats. Motorboats cause repeated waves which damage the banks, while sewage release into the waters increases eutrophication (see page 25).

SAQ 5.1

Give three reasons why National Parks face major conservation issues.

Other government conservation measures

National Nature Reserves

National Nature Reserves (**NNRs**) are smaller and more numerous than National Parks. They are areas of national importance for the protection of biological diversity, managed as nature reserves by English Nature, Scottish Natural Heritage, the Countryside Council for Wales and the Environment and Heritage Agency for Northern Ireland. By 1999 there were a total of 333 NNRs in England, Scotland and Wales (*table 5.1* on page 54). They are identified specifically because of their importance in protecting biodiversity in Britain. The definitive account of the functions of National Nature Reserves in Britain, published in 1977 by the then Nature Conservancy Council, identified four functions *in addition* to conservation:

- research;
- demonstration and advice;
- education;
- amenity and access.

These four functions need not conflict with conservation. Indeed, given a sympathetic landowner and intelligent management, they can support and enhance conservation. However, landowners can change and not all are sympathetic to conservation. So although National Nature Reserves benefit from very strong protection under the law, they do not enjoy a guaranteed and protected future.

Environmentally Sensitive Areas

Because the National Parks were designated with wild, open places in mind, this left many lowland areas of beauty with no monitoring or protection of the scenery. The European Community prompted change in 1985 with a regulation about promoting national schemes to aid farmers in important ecological and landscape areas. So in 1987 the category of **Environmentally Sensitive Area** (**ESA**) was introduced by the Minister of Agriculture in fulfilment

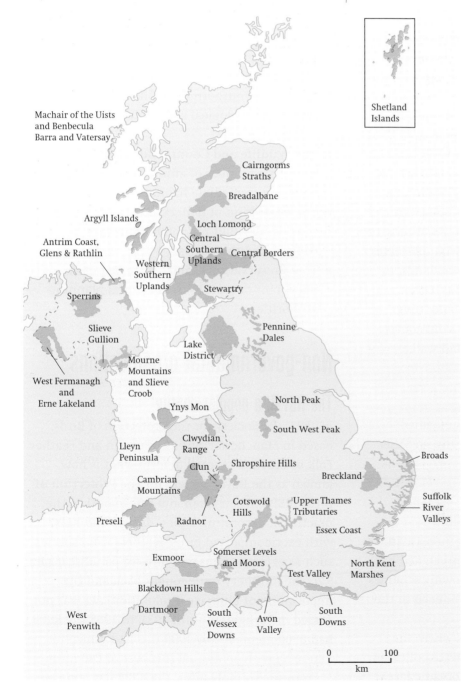

● **Figure 5.6** Environmentally Sensitive Areas (ESAs) in the UK.

of the following criteria: 'Areas of national environmental significance whose conservation depends on the adoption, maintenance or extension of a particular form of farming practice; in which there have occurred, or there is a likelihood of, changes in farming practices which pose a major threat to the environment; which represent a discrete and coherent unit of environmental interest; and which would permit the economic administration of appropriate conservation aids.'

In other words, there are areas in the UK whose beauty is considered to be the result of particular farming methods. If these methods change, then the appeal of the area may be lessened. Because of this there are often restrictions on the amounts of fertilisers and pesticides which can be used and the time of year they can be applied. These vary from ESA to ESA depending on the history of the landscape involved. In 1999 there were a total of 43 ESAs in the UK including 22 ESAs in England (*figure 5.6*).

In ESAs farmers are paid to manage their land so as to conserve features created by traditional land-use management. For example, some farmers are paid to keep sheep when this would otherwise be unprofitable for them. Sheep grazing preserves grassland (see pages 10–11). Chalk grasslands, in particular, are rich in beautiful plants. Other farmers are paid not to drain their land, thus enabling water meadows and other semi-aquatic habitats to be retained. Hedgerow and wall maintenance are also supported.

SAQ 5.2

Without quoting extended definitions of either, summarise the essential differences between SSSIs and ESAs.

Other UK legislation protecting wildlife

Recent years have seen a significant increase in UK government legislation to protect threatened habitats or endangered species. The following schemes or pieces of legislation were all introduced in the 1980s or 1990s:

■ **Nitrate Vulnerable Zones** – areas where the water courses are at risk from nitrate pollution; storage and use of chemical and organic fertilisers are controlled by laws originating in the European Community Nitrate Directive.

■ **Heritage Coasts** – undeveloped coastline, defined by the Countryside Agency, specified in local authority structure plans and benefiting from management funding. Most are SSSIs and within National Parks.

■ **Farm Woodland Scheme** – a European Union (EU) scheme in which financial incentives encourage landowners to plant trees.

■ **Set-aside** – an EU scheme of grants given to farmers to take at least 20% of their land out of arable production and leave the fields uncultivated.

■ **Areas of Outstanding Natural Beauty** (AONBs) – aimed at preserving beautiful landscapes in intensively farmed areas, especially the countryside's attractiveness, including buildings. About half are in Southern England and most contain important ecological sites which are designated SSSIs.

■ **The Wildlife and Countryside Act** (**1981**) – protects a number of animal and plant species and their immediate habitats.

■ **The Protection of Badgers Act** (**1992**) – provides considerable (but not total) protection to badgers and their setts.

■ **Tree Preservation Orders** – can be put on important or mature trees by local planning authorities.

Non-governmental organisations

The RSPB: a popular charity

In 1891, the Society for the Protection of Birds, based in Manchester, and the Fur, Fin and Feather Folk of Croydon merged to form what is now known as the **Royal Society for the Protection of Birds (RSPB)**. Their main aim was to outlaw the practice of decorating ladies' dresses and hats with exotic imported birds' feathers from species such as egrets, herons and birds of paradise (*figure 5.7*). The millinery trade fought back and the Importation of Plumage (Prohibition) Act was not passed in Parliament until 1921. In 1958 the RSPB had 8000 members; by 1999 this had grown to 1 004 000, with an annual turnover of £40 million.

From such simple aims, the RSPB has gone on to purchase and manage some 150 nature reserves

● **Figure 5.7** The story of the egret paraded through the streets of London in July 1911 by men employed by the Royal Society for the Protection of Birds. Board titles include 'The Badge of Cruelty!', 'The Dead Mother' and 'Crying for Food!'.

■ educating through environmental education publications and the activities of its **Wildlife Explorers** and **RSPB Phoenix** clubs – for example, a newsletter called Sixth Sense aimed at 16- to 19-year-olds is sent to all schools each term.

The RSPB organises annual bird surveys such as the Big Garden Birdwatch: individuals (over 27 000 in January, 1999) take part by watching their garden or a nearby area on an appointed day and recording which bird species visit. The annual changes in abundance of different bird species provide vital information about which birds are thriving and which are declining. Some birds, such as starlings, blackbirds and blue-tits, thrive in the urban environment while others, like song thrushes, are doing less well. The 1994 survey recorded only about half the song thrushes seen in 1979. This is probably mainly due to lack of food (slugs and snails) in over-controlled gardens and farmland. Regular monitoring of wildlife

of over 100 000 hectares for the benefit of birds, and therefore other organisms as well. Most reserves are stunningly beautiful and the visitor is almost guaranteed views of rare birds such as avocets, ospreys, marsh harriers, stone curlews or choughs. The accent has slowly shifted from conservation of individual bird species to whole ecosystems. Their attractive quarterly journal increasingly has information about small furry mammals, insects and plant life.

In addition to purchasing and managing reserves, the RSPB is engaged in many other activities including:

■ fund-raising for various projects, helped by effective publicity (e.g. *figure 5.8*);

■ providing evidence for the prosecution of egg collectors and people who poison birds of prey;

■ lobbying members of parliament on conservation and farming issues;

■ fighting development proposals that threaten valuable habitats;

■ campaigning against such things as large scale peat extraction and illegal trade in wild birds;

■ researching, both in this country and overseas, the survival and reproduction of birds which live in or visit Britain;

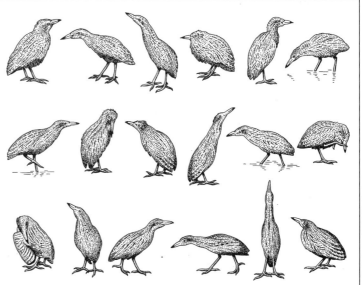

There are only this many breeding male bitterns alive in Britain today...

● **Figure 5.8** A 1993 RSPB campaign on behalf of bitterns, whose numbers remain perilously small: in 1999 there were 19 breeding males.

abundance is important as it reveals the trends. Loss of farmland birds over the last 25 years (skylarks, grey partridges and turtle doves are all down by 75% or more) has helped draw attention to the effects of the changing farming practices described in chapter 2.

The RSPB is developing increasingly wider roles. It now links with other environmental organisations to lobby the UK parliaments and assemblies for tougher wildlife protection laws. The RSPB is a key partner in the UK Biodiversity Action Plans, drawn up by agreement between Government agencies, non-government organisations, (NGOs) and landowners as part of the UK's environmental obligations from the Rio Earth Summit in 1992. By 1999 the RSPB had responsibility for 30 of the 400 species designated as being at risk. Obviously most are birds, but there are also six insects, two lichens and a plant. Recently the RSPB has provided experts to sit on committees investigating the impact of genetically modified crops on biodiversity, and has produced reports on subjects such as the future of livestock farming and the EU Common Agricultural Policy. It has many international links for the conservation of birds and habitats overseas.

The RSPB can be contacted at The Lodge, Sandy, Bedfordshire, SG19 2DL. Tel. 01767 680551. Website: www.rspb.org.uk

SAQ 5.3

To the nearest whole number, what percentage of people in the UK are members of the RSPB? (You may like to look back at page 5.)

Other voluntary conservation bodies

Voluntary societies play an important role in conservation in the UK. The best way to assure the survival of a habitat is by buying it to manage as a reserve: the government legislation is not strong enough to trust it to protect designated sites sufficiently. Because naturalist societies are voluntary they rely on funding from the general public to carry out their programmes of conservation. There are many ways you can help such societies. You can become a member, visit the local reserves, help in fund-raising, take part in surveys and even,

if the opportunity arises, help to manage a reserve. Surveys organised by voluntary conservation bodies have included rook watches, National Dormouse Week (hunts for nuts opened by dormice), otter surveys and a survey of what cats catch – the threat to wildlife from some cats is considerable.

One exciting and relatively new charity is **The Woodland Trust**. This is growing rapidly, probably because it seems to have captured the public imagination for its mixture of conservation and habitat creation. The Woodland Trust was founded in 1972 by Kenneth Watkins because he saw the need for an organisation to acquire and manage smaller broad-leaved woods. It quickly became one of Britain's fastest growing conservation groups. The Trust's aim 'is to safeguard trees, small areas as well as large, by raising money to buy and look after woods that might otherwise be destroyed and to plant trees to create new woods'.

In 1999 the Woodland Trust obtained its 1000th wood and now manages 17 200 hectares, nearly twice the 1993 area, and almost all open to the public. It has an annual income of £14 million and 61 000 members. It has set out 11 woodland management principles 'in order to convey a clear understanding of the way in which we seek to manage our woods to all those who support our work'. They are as follows:

1 The Woodland Trust invites its members and the general public into its woods for informal recreation and quiet enjoyment. Safety is paramount, and will be secured before any Trust woods are opened to visitors.

2 The Trust provides and maintains footpaths, gates, stiles and similar low-level facilities for public access to a level appropriate to the degree of use of each property.

3 The public benefit of the Trust's woods lies principally in their aesthetic qualities – beauty, tranquillity, timelessness – and in their value for wildlife.

4 In caring for and conserving its woods, the primary aim of the Trust's silvicultural management is therefore to preserve these qualities by following and emulating natural processes as far as possible. This includes the retention, where appropriate, of old trees to full maturity and death.

5 Before taking any action the Trust considers carefully if it is necessary. The broad-leaved timescale is measured in decades and there is very rarely any hurry to intervene.

6 If it is necessary to intervene the work will be as little and as unobtrusive as possible.

7 It is essential to understand clearly the long-term consequences of intervention and ensure that work is carried out in accordance with these principles.

8 Where we carry out any works in our woods we wish to achieve this in the most economical and effective manner possible but with full consideration of good woodland management practice.

9 The Trust does not make market-driven decisions but wherever possible costs of management operations will be minimised by imaginative and effective marketing.

10 We seek to explain our operations in advance and the support of the local community will be actively encouraged.

11 In assuming responsibility for the care of our woods in perpetuity, the Trust also recognises the obligations of ownership both as a landowner and as a neighbour.

The Woodland Trust can be contacted at Autumn Park, Grantham, Lincolnshire NG31 6LL. Tel. 01476 581111. Website: www.woodland-trust.org.uk

Another nationwide conservation organisation is **The Wildlife Trusts**, a partnership of 46 local Wildlife Trusts. This is one of the major voluntary organisations with over 2300 nature reserves around the country. Total membership exceeds 320 000 people. The Wildlife Trusts aim to manage the reserves on sustainable principles and to enrich the wildlife of the UK. It has a junior branch called Wildlife Watch and 52 Urban Wildlife Groups. Each local trust has many conservation and social activities.

The address of the central office for The Wildlife Trusts is: The Kiln, Mather Road, Newark NG24 1WT. Tel. 01636 677711. Website: www.wildlifetrust.org.uk

The British Trust for Conservation Volunteers (BTCV) is a useful group to contact if you are interested in getting actively involved in conservation. They run hundreds of practical courses each year on topics such as dry stone walling, hedge laying and pond cleaning as well as providing Natural Break working holidays for over-16s. They also run a school membership scheme giving advice about conservation in school grounds. The BTCV have contacts and local offices in almost every county, but their main office is: The British Trust for Conservation Volunteers, 36 St Mary's Street, Wallingford, Oxfordshire OX10 0EU. Tel. 01491 839766. Website: www.btcv.org.uk

SUMMARY

- Sites of Special Scientific Interest (SSSIs) are areas of particular scientific importance in the UK.
- A National Park is an area of substantial size and outstandingly attractive scenery in England or Wales that is specially protected and reserved for public enjoyment.
- National Parks face a number of major conservation issues.
- Environmentally Sensitive Areas (ESAs) are areas of national environmental significance in England or Wales whose conservation depends on particular farming practices.
- Non-government organisations play a crucial role in nature conservation in the UK.
- The Royal Society for the Protection of Birds (RSPB) is one of the biggest nature conservation bodies in the UK.

Questions

1 Describe the different ways in which land may be protected in England or Wales for the purposes of nature conservation.

2 Discuss the major conservation issues faced by a named National Park.

3 Describe the role of the Royal Society for the Protection of Birds (RSPB).

CHAPTER 6

International conservation issues

By the end of this chapter you should be able to:

1 describe the role of zoos and botanic gardens with regard to captive breeding and release programmes and the preservation of seed banks;

2 discuss the Convention on International Trade in Endangered Species of Wild Fauna and Flora (CITES) and the problems in its implementation;

3 discuss the conservation of the African elephant with regard to population numbers, reasons for concern, measures introduced and international co-operation required;

4 discuss the conservation of tropical rainforest with regard to ecological importance, reasons for decline and international measures that need to be, or are being, taken.

Global issues

Many of the issues involved in conservation are global in nature and require international co-operation. The need to reduce pollution and to maintain biodiversity affects everyone wherever they live. We have already looked at farming, global warming, pollution of the atmosphere and oceans, overfishing, deforestation and human population growth. In this chapter we return to the threats to biodiversity caused by human activities that directly endanger species, and examine the difficulties involved in saving species from extinction.

Ever since life evolved, species have gone extinct. Extinction is a 'natural' phenomenon and there are probably very many reasons and combinations of reasons why species go extinct, including competition from other species, gradual changes in sea level or climate, and sudden changes caused by natural catastrophes such as meteor impacts or volcanic eruptions. However, the risk of extinction has increased greatly due to human activity. Many species are now at risk from habitat loss, hunting (e.g. fishing), damage to communities by introduced species, loss of disease resistance caused by pollution and, perhaps in the

future, global warming and other forms of climate change. Habitat loss is perhaps the most serious threat as whole communities can be lost in one go. The tropical forests are facing this threat right now (see pages 70–73). Just think of the world before humans developed agriculture, then think of all the land cleared for farms, cities, industries and transport and you can imagine how great is the loss of natural communities.

Once an animal or plant is rare, it is at extra risk: parrots and exotic orchids are good examples of species under threat from collectors. The unusually shaped lady's slipper orchid (*Cypripedium calceolus*) is now very rare all over Europe (*figure 6.1*). The UK form is a darker subspecies, which now survives as a few flowering spikes at one secret and protected site in one of our National Parks. Plant propagation specialists have been trying to increase the plant numbers by cloning tissue cultures. Yet one of the authors remembers talking with an old lady whose boyfriend once picked her 'a bunch' of these flowers!

Sometimes a product from an organism will command a high price as a status symbol or as a

● **Figure 6.1** The rarest plant in Britain? The lady's slipper orchid (*Cypripedium calceolus*).

source of folk medicine. Examples include elephant ivory (discussed on pages 68–69), wildcat skins, tiger parts and rhinoceros horns. Determined poachers with guns intent on killing an endangered animal for massive profits are very difficult to stop and international control in the trade of such animals or plants is the best method of prevention (see pages 67–68). Sometimes when a species is very rare it may have to be conserved in captivity and this is where zoological and botanical gardens become important.

The roles of zoos and botanic gardens in conservation

Zoos

Zoos have three main aims: conservation, education and research. They also need to attract visitors: a zoo that fails to get enough people through its doors soon closes. Zoos and wildlife parks often have large, spectacular mammals such as big cats, elephants, bears or something very rare, like a giant panda, to pull in the crowds. There was a time when animals were bred in zoos mainly because the public liked to see the young animals. Now every good zoo, however small, has at least one **captive breeding programme** in which a rare

or endangered species is bred in captivity. Captive breeding programmes have the following benefits:

- Fewer animals need to be caught in the wild to supply zoos, thus reducing animal suffering;
- Reduced pressure on the wild stock reduces the chances of extinction;
- Successful captive breeding may enable a species to be **reintroduced** into the wild.

A good example of captive breeding and release is the rescue of the Nene goose (*Branta sandvicensis*), the largest native bird of Hawaii. In this island habitat the birds clamber about on the sparsely vegetated volcanic slopes, so their feet have larger toes and less webbing than other geese. They are less vocal than their mainland relatives and emit a low mournful moan. Uniquely among northern geese, the species is non-migratory: the result of living on an isolated island chain.

In the nineteenth century there were over 20 000 Nene geese in the Hawaiian islands. By the late 1940s there were only about 40. Their drastic decline was mostly the result of the introduction of non-native terrestrial predators: the dog, the rat and, most of all, the mongoose. These animals found the goose and its eggs easy prey. Ironically, the mongoose had only been introduced in the hope that it would control the rats – another example of biological control gone wrong (see page 23).

In a desperate attempt to save the bird, two females and a male were sent, in 1951, to the **Wildfowl and Wetlands Trust** in England, founded by Sir Peter Scott in 1946. Initially, breeding success was low, but with time better results were achieved and by the end of the 1970s there were a total of 1200 Nene geese in wildfowl sanctuaries around the world, while some 1600 had been released back into Hawaii (*figure 6.2*). Here they have successfully re-established themselves, due to efforts to control their predators, and netting has been put around their nesting sites to stop the mongooses and rats getting to the eggs.

The Nene goose story is not unique. A number of other species have been rescued from extinction through captive breeding and reintroduction to the wild. Examples include the golden lion tamarin (a small monkey found only in coastal forests of the state of Rio de Janeiro in Brazil) and the Arabian oryx (a large gazelle-like herbivore

● **Figure 6.2** The Nene goose, saved from extinction through captive breeding. This is a ringed bird, back in its native Hawaiian habitat.

found in semi-desert scrub in the Middle East). Releasing captive-bred animals does have problems. Animals are sometimes too tame or too used to captivity to survive on their own. They may have difficulty obtaining food, or be too frightened to cope with a strange environment. Some species, elephants for example, know where to get salt and how to find water in severe droughts, but only within their family area. However, captive breeding experts are constantly improving their preparation of animals to be released. Another problem is that the original threat, such as poaching or an efficient predator, may still endanger the animals after release.

Despite these successes it must be realised that out of some 15 million different species of animal on Earth, a third are at risk of extinction by the year 2025. Captive breeding can only play a tiny part in helping to conserve all these species.

Successful captive breeding is both an art and a science. For such programmes to work they need people with an excellent knowledge of the biology of the species and people with perseverance and a love for the animal so that they keep going when little success seems to be forthcoming. Adequate funding is a necessity too. Where a species is very rare, there is a terrible risk to capturing and removing most, or all, of the remaining animals from the wild to start the captive breeding programme. If the animals fail to breed, the workers will not have saved that species but will have hastened its extinction.

Every captive breeding programme must consider the problem of **inbreeding**. Inbreeding

happens when closely related individuals, for example a brother and a sister, mate. Some species naturally inbreed in the wild. For these species, inbreeding in captivity poses few problems. However, most species usually outbreed with mates that are only distantly related or not related. When individuals from these species inbreed, the offspring are much less likely to survive and reproduce successfully. The reason for this **inbreeding depression** is that inbreeding greatly increases the chances of an individual inheriting the same harmful recessive alleles from both parents. Resulting offspring will be homozygous for harmful recessive alleles at one or more of their gene loci. As a result they may lack vital gene products and be less likely to survive and reproduce successfully.

Because of the dangers of inbreeding, zoos nowadays keep careful records detailing the family trees of all their animals. This allows them to ensure that individuals that mate are as distantly related as possible. Zoos often swap animals with other zoos to promote outbreeding. Encouraging outbreeding of individuals around the world maintains the genetic diversity of the captive populations. Such diversity is important if groups of animals are eventually to be returned to the wild.

Of course the phrase 'captive breeding' suggests the animals in captivity *will* breed successfully. Often it is very difficult to get animals to reproduce in an unnatural situation, on unusual foods and in a strange climate and environment. Many species have a complex behaviour of mate choice and rearing young. Simply providing a mate choosen to reduce inbreeding may not be acceptable to the animals concerned. Despite all a zoo's best efforts, such captive animals may exhibit considerable stress and atypical behaviour (such as 'pacing' in carnivores when they pad round and round their enclosure). Such stress may make them more susceptible to disease when in captivity, or conversely they may catch diseases when released that were not present in the zoo.

Arguably, captive breeding of animals only has a long-term value if their wild habitats still exist for them to be reintroduced to. Is there a value in captive breeding if the populations remain in zoos forever?

SAQ 6.1

What sorts of species do zoos keep so as to attract members of the general public?

SAQ 6.2

What sorts of species can zoos do most to help by captive breeding?

Botanic gardens

The earliest botanic gardens were created many centuries ago in China, in prehistoric Mexico and in the Arab world. The first European botanic garden followed much later, being founded in Pisa in 1543. In the sixteenth and seventeenth centuries the main function of European botanic gardens was to grow plants of medicinal value for the training of medical students. The focus of research then shifted to taxonomic studies in the eighteenth century. Today botanic gardens have many functions and conservation is an important one of them.

Botanic gardens can do a tremendous amount for conservation. While London Zoo houses only 900 species of animals, the Royal Botanic Gardens at Kew boast 40 000 of the world's 300 000 species of vascular plants! It is easier and cheaper to keep a plant than an animal. One of the useful things about many plants is that their seeds can be kept alive for years. Careful reduction of the moisture content under conditions of low temperature followed by freezing, preserves the seeds, sometimes for hundreds of years. Such **seed banks** play a vital role in conservation (*figure 6.3*). As the result of a special grant, Kew has established a Millennium Seed Bank, which is an important addition to its collection of world floras.

Some seed banks specialise in preserving different varieties of crop plants, which maintains a gene reservoir for the breeding of future varieties. The importance of conserving crop varieties cannot be overestimated. The genetic uniformity of many of the world's food plants is very worrying. To date, disaster has largely been avoided through the application of huge quantities of pesticides. However, every few years much of the yield from one or other variety of wheat, potato, maize or other food crop is lost as a result of the evolution of a new strain of insect, fungus or virus. As many countries now rely on only a handful of crop varieties there is always the risk that one year most of the harvest of a country might fail.

Many tropical plants, including a number of important crops, produce seed that can only be stored for a few weeks or months. For these species a seed bank is impractical. An alternative is to grow the different varieties of the adult plants year after year, ensuring that pollination occurs only within the variety to keep it genetically pure. The problem with this procedure is the space, time and effort involved. Crops maintained this way include cocoa, rubber, coconut, mango, cassava and yam.

SAQ 6.3

a What percentage of the world's animal species does London Zoo house?

b What percentage of the world's vascular plants do the Royal Botanic Gardens at Kew house?

● **Figure 6.3** Part of the cold storage seed bank at Wellesbourne, Warwickshire.

Trade in endangered species

CITES

CITES stands for the **Convention on International Trade in Endangered Species of Wild Fauna and Flora**. It was signed in Washington in 1973 as an international agreement to monitor and control the trade in endangered species. The 145th country (Azerbaijan) joined CITES in February 1999.

CITES has drawn up several lists or 'appendixes' of species for which there is an international trade and which are considered to be in danger of extinction.

- **Appendix I** contains species threatened with extinction. No international trade is allowed in living or dead material. An export licence *can* be obtained, but only if an import licence from the country of import has been given on the basis of scientific evidence that the trade will not harm the survival of the species.

- **Appendix II** contains species that may be threatened with extinction in the future if trade in them is not strictly regulated. An export licence is required which is issued if the export is not harmful to the survival of the species.

- **Appendix III** contains species that a particular country feels need protection and where the co-operation of other countries is needed to control international trade. Any trade requires either an export licence from the country concerned or a certificate of origin to state that the traded items have not originated in that country.

Appendix I usually contains individually named species; Appendix II may contain whole families, for example all cacti, all orchids (but not cultivated cut flowers) and all cycads (a group of tough-leaved, non-flowering seed plants). Use of Appendix III is rare and depends on which countries request it. For example, Nepal asked for a few rare tree species to be put on Appendix III. In fact, Nepal has fewer endangered species than most countries in the world, yet these other countries seem reluctant to use Appendix III. Many countries have stricter laws than CITES and require import permits for all Appendix II species. The EU, for example, treats some Appendix II species as if they were on Appendix I – for instance, no trade is allowed in any orchids native to Europe (*figure 6.1* shows one example).

There are a number of problems in the implementation of CITES. Indeed, it has been estimated that the illegal trade in endangered species is worth many billions of dollars a year. One problem is the identification of listed species; it is asking rather a lot of customs officials to be able to identify all these to the level required. Another problem is the level of policing in different countries; in many places illegally obtained goods are sold openly. Many of the problems of protecting an endangered species are illustrated by the particular example of the African elephant.

Conservation of the African elephant

In the nineteenth century there were probably between 5 and 10 million African elephants, *Loxodonta africana* (*figure 6.4*). By 1970 there were probably still three million, but this had plunged to about 500 000 by the end of 1993, with the worst hit areas losing 85% or more of their elephants. As the biologist Colin Tudge has written of the elephant situation 'A crisis quickly degenerates into a cliché as people lose interest, yet the crisis persists'.

Until the 1960s the elephant populations of Africa were thriving. Many elephants were shot when they encroached onto farmland and some elephants were killed for the ivory obtained from their tusks. Yet overall numbers were healthy. In the early 1970s the price of ivory soared in response to a growing demand from Asian countries. Prices for ivory increased until by the late 1980s ivory sold for $200–300 a kilogram on the open market – more than the price of silver. Only some 10% of this went

● **Figure 6.4** A matriarchal family of African elephants.

to the poachers, but in many African countries $300 is a good annual income.

The decline in numbers does not tell the whole tragedy. Both males and females have tusks and the animals with the largest tusks are adults. Consequently mainly adults are killed: in some areas there are no adults left. As elephants live in social groups led by mothers – elephant societies are matriarchal – young elephants now often lack the teaching and guidance that normally comes from older females. Troops of young delinquent elephants can be seen aimlessly roaming the savannah. It is unclear what they will be like as parents, should they ever survive to adulthood.

In 1986 quotas for ivory export were set by CITES which were based on what each country's elephant population was able to sustain. However, the system was widely abused and poaching, often using automatic rifles, was widespread.

In 1990 CITES responded by placing the African elephant on Appendix I, thus banning all international trade in tusks. The international market for ivory virtually collapsed and the price fell significantly as a result. Encouragingly, elephant numbers rapidly recovered to 580 000 by 1995. Countries with elephants benefit from tourist income in addition to the many valuable products, including ivory, meat and elephant hide, that can be obtained directly from the animal in carefully controlled culls. Wildlife tourism has become an important source of income for many tropical countries in recent years, and the term **ecotourism** has been coined to refer to this.

Most countries have seen preservation as the way to conserve elephants. A different approach was taken by Zimbabwe, which refused to support the 1990 CITES ban on the international trade in ivory. Instead it opted for a policy of management. Zimbabwe argued that even in 1990, there were more elephants in the country than the habitat could sustain. Accordingly, it set its own quotas, culled elephants and allowed ivory to be traded.

Zimbabwe's elephant policy has been part of a larger strategy aimed at managing wildlife as a valuable resource. Its CAMPFIRE programme, started in 1987, allows rural communities to benefit from the wildlife on communal lands. The communal lands are often adjacent to the 15% of

Zimbabwe that is protected as National Parks or forest reserves. Before CAMPFIRE, rural communities often saw large wildlife as a threat that came out of the reserves and damaged their crops and livelihoods. Now some species are exploited for their meat, others for their hides or other products, but most (about 90%) of the revenue from wildlife comes from safari hunting by rich foreigners who will pay many thousands of pounds to shoot an elephant, leopard or other large animal. About 100 bull elephants are taken each year by trophy hunters and another 30 shot because they are causing problems around farmsteads. Before CAMPFIRE started, 50 bull elephants a year were taken for trophies, but as many as 200–300 were shot by farmers. So the programme has actually *reduced* elephant killing by making the community more reluctant to kill animals raiding their crops because of their value as trophies. The amount of land given over to wildlife has also increased dramatically – up from 12% of the country in 1988 to 33% in 1998 – because the economic returns from wildlife now exceed those from cattle.

Even if the time comes when African elephants are no longer killed for their ivory, they may still be endangered. Everywhere the growth in human population threatens their habitats. Empowering local people to manage and profit from their own wildlife seems to be a very positive and successful way of conserving ecosystems in a sustainable way. Several other African countries are now following Zimbabwe's lead. The battle between wildlife and human populations for land and resources must be converted into a willingness by local people to preserve their wildlife, otherwise the humans will win every time at the expense of our global biodiversity.

In 1997, the 138 nations then in CITES agreed that in 1999, the African elephant should be removed from Appendix I in Botswana, Namibia and Zimbabwe. This was only allowed because the three countries convinced CITES that they had set up adequate measures to prevent poaching, including a means of tracing and identifying tusks to prevent the laundering of illegally obtained ivory through the legal systems. Initially only stockpiles of ivory could be sold. It is too soon to tell what the effects will be of this change in policy, although concern has been expressed that anything that makes ivory control more difficult or less effective might well encourage poaching. Indeed there is some early and worrying evidence of an increase in poaching in other African countries such as Kenya.

Before we leave the African elephant we should mention that poachers' attentions have now also turned to its relative, the Asian elephant, *Elephas maximus*. This species has long enjoyed a symbiotic relationship with humans, being almost semi-domesticated in some places. The Asian elephant was listed on Appendix I by CITES much earlier than the African, in 1975. All Asian elephants are born in the wild, which makes them vulnerable to forest clearance as well as to poachers. Total numbers are thought to have fallen from 50 000 worldwide in 1993 to 35 000 in 1997.

SAQ 6.4

List four arguments in favour of the conservation of the African elephant.

Ecosystem conservation

The importance of ecosystems

So far we have only looked at the survival of individual animal and plant species either in zoos, seed banks or in the wild. However, all the hard work of conservationists in these areas would come to nothing if the ecosystems these species come from disappear. In the past, much stress has been placed on saving particular species from extinction: the giant panda, whales, the tiger, the African elephant and so on. Each of these species has much effort and money spent on it by a relatively small number of dedicated people.

You may have noticed that most of the species that get publicity are large and magnificent or small and cuddly or have attractive flowers. Yet all these species come from ecosystems containing hundreds or thousands of species. The future of conservation now is surely in the preservation, or if needs be, creation of ecosystems. Many of these are now extremely rare, fragmented or damaged; others which seem abundant (tropical forest, for example) are disappearing at an alarming rate.

Tropical rainforests

Tropical rainforests require a hot climate and abundant rainfall throughout the year. They are found near the equator in South and Central America, West and Equatorial Africa, South-east Asia, Indonesia and North-east Australia. The combination of year-round warmth and moisture allows continuous plant growth to occur. The result is that **plant productivity** is extremely high and the plants are evergreen (they retain leaves throughout the year). High plant productivity and a relatively constant climate result in a tremendous diversity of life.

Tropical rainforests are the most diverse and spectacular of all ecosystems (*figure 6.5*). Indeed there are probably as many different species of organisms within them as there are in the whole of

Figure 6.5 The biodiversity of the Amazon tropical rainforest is higher than anywhere else on Earth. This is in French Guiana on the northern edge of the Amazon basin.

	Area (× 10⁶ ha)	Vascular plant species	Species per km²
Tropical forests			
Central and South American	400	90 000	0.025
African	180	30 000	0.017
Indo-Malayan	250	35 000	0.014
Temperate forests			
British Isles	30	1438	0.0048
US	737	20 000	0.0027

● **Table 6.1** Land area and vascular plant diversity in the three regions of tropical rainforest. Data for the temperate forests of the British Isles and US are added for comparison.

● **Figure 6.7** Three-toed sloth carrying its young.

the rest of the world put together. Their biodiversity is very high because they have large numbers of tree species, often 100–300 per hectare. The wetter the climate, the more diverse the forest. South American rainforests are the largest and most diverse (*table 6.1*). Most of the species they contain have not even been named, let alone studied.

At ground level some tropical rainforests can be surprisingly easy to walk through. This is because little light reaches the forest floor. Most of it is trapped in the **canopy**, some 30–50 m up. Many tall trees carry **epiphytes** (plants that grow on other, larger plants) and **lianas** (climbing plants that use the trees to support their growth into the

canopy) (*figure 6.6*). Nutrient cycling within the canopy is important, and many plants possess aerial roots that absorb water and nutrients, just as soil roots do. The nutrients drip down from leaves in the canopy and come from the decomposition of dead animals and their faeces. In the rainforest, flowers and fruits are found throughout the year and provide nourishment for birds, mammals and countless insects and other invertebrates.

Other animals are specialist leaf eaters (*figure 6.7*). Sloths, for example, have large multi-compartmented stomachs that hold cellulose-digesting bacteria. These enable the sloths to break down tough leaves. Even so, food may spend a month in the stomach before passing into the intestines for absorption. Living on such an indigestible diet has many consequences for a sloth's ecology. Sloths are, of course, notoriously slow. Their body temperature is low for a mammal, about 30–34 °C, and variable, falling each night, during wet weather and when the animal is even less active than usual. These strategies all help conserve energy. Their slow lifestyle means they cannot run away from predators. Camouflage is therefore important and is provided by two species of

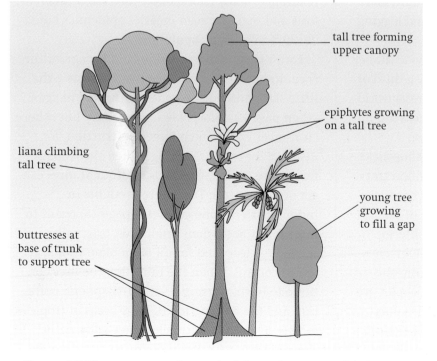

liana climbing tall tree

buttresses at base of trunk to support tree

tall tree forming upper canopy

epiphytes growing on a tall tree

young tree growing to fill a gap

● **Figure 6.6** The structure of a tropical forest (compare with *figure 6.5*).

cyanobacteria (blue-green bacteria), which live on their fur and turn it green. There are a lot of leaves in a rainforest and the sloth lifestyle has been successful; sloths are the most abundant large mammals in tropical South American forests.

Although tropical rainforests are very productive, almost all the nutrients are tied up in the organisms themselves. Decomposition is so rapid that the soils contain little organic matter or minerals. As a consequence, removal of the vegetation, by logging or burning, rarely leads to successful agriculture. Within a few years crops fail, and so the farmer is forced to move on and clear another patch of land (*figure 2.3* on page 12).

The tropical rainforests are so vast and so diverse that, as yet, we know all too little about their ecology. Their very importance for global biodiversity suggests they should be cherished rather than exploited ruthlessly, yet tropical rainforests face many pressures from humans and are under serious threat of destruction. They suffer greatly from **deforestation** – between 1972 and 1998 the Amazon basin lost at least 532 000 km^2, that is over 13% of its entire forest. This figure was calculated using satellite imaging (*figure 6.8*), which clearly showed the loss and fragmentation of the forest. Satellite imaging does not detect cleared areas of less than 5 km^2, so the 13% figure cited above is almost certainly an underestimate. An additional 10 000–15 000 km^2 are damaged by fire and logging each year.

Tropical rainforests are logged to provide timber for export. Japan imports approximately a third of the wood exported from tropical rainforests worldwide. Once it reaches Japan, much of the wood is used for chopsticks or in the construction industry. You might think the need for chopsticks is not important – but China fells 25 million trees a year to produce 45 billion disposable chopsticks!

Forest is cleared for the construction of roads, which let subsistence farmers into the interior. The roads develop characteristic 'side-shoot' clearings (*figure 6.8*). These farmers are not from the indigenous peoples of the forest; such peoples are all too often forcibly removed from their lands. Other incomers include miners, there to exploit the rich deposits of heavy metals, especially gold. Mining introduces pollution to the forest and

● **Figure 6.8** Landsat satellite image of about 240 km^2 of Rondonia, Western Brazil, taken in 1988. Tropical forest appears greenish–brown in colour, swampy savannah (mostly bottom left) is a rich blue. Two types of deforestation are apparent: the pale blue squares and rectangles (upper centre) are large scale logging; the fuzzier blue grid (bottom right) are numerous small 'slash and burn' clearances clustered along road systems.

river systems, thus further damaging the ecosystem. Miners have carried several diseases into the forest to which the native Amazonians had no resistance. Many tribespeople died from tuberculosis and malaria; even measles epidemics killed 20–30 % of village populations.

Forest clearance to provide land for agriculture is common. Much clearance is small-scale – the little slash and burn patches illustrated in *figure 2.3* on page 12 and visible in *figure 6.8* – but other clearances cause much larger destruction, for instance for cattle ranching. When the tropical forests are suffering periods of drought, fires can get out of control. The severe droughts in Indonesia in El Niño years (see page 38) result in huge forest fires when small fires, originally started to clear land for oil palm plantations, get out of control. When the rains fail, the fires continue to burn, causing severe atmospheric pollution and the destruction of large areas of tropical forests. Even small farm clearance adds up, as shown in *figure 6.8*. Sadly the nutrient-poor soils are usually unsuitable for the cultivation of agricultural crops. In Zaire, for example, the yield of cassava in the second year of cultivation on forest soil is only about 65% of the yield in the first year of cultivation. For rice the figure is 25%, and for peanuts just 15%. The same problem occurs in ranching; cattle in the Amazon basin can develop brittle bones because of the poor quality of grazing.

So why should we save the tropical rainforests? As always, there are ethical and economic arguments:

- Do humans have the right to cause millions of species to become extinct? After all, extinction is forever.
- Destruction of tropical forests will contribute towards global warming, increasing the risk of disastrous climate changes (see page 38).
- Many drugs undoubtedly await discovery and isolation from rainforest plants.
- Rainforests can provide sustainable crops of nuts, fruits, rubber, honey and vegetable oils, more valuable in the long term than the short-term profits from logging and clearing.
- Forests increase the water content of the atmosphere by transpiration. Destroying tropical rainforests decreases rainfall in the tropics.
- Deforestation often leads to **soil erosion**. Normally the dense vegetation prevents even heavy rains from washing away the soil. The plants in a rainforest act rather like a sponge, holding onto water and only gradually releasing it into the rivers. Without the plants, floods occur and thousands of years of soil accumulation may be lost within a few weeks. Mudslides can engulf whole villages within minutes.

● **Figure 6.9** Chico Mendes, a rubber-tapper who fought to save the Brazilian forests and was murdered as a result.

At the same time, it must be realised that the forces currently causing the destruction of tropical rainforests are *economic* ones. Brazil, for example, is not a wealthy country, except for the richest 10% of the population. Much of the country's much-needed foreign currency derives directly from the destruction of its forests as they are opened up to ranchers, loggers of hardwood timbers such as mahogany, wood pulp producers and miners. Opposition within Brazil to habitat destruction is often dangerous. Chico Mendes (*figure 6.9*) was a rubber-tapper and the founder and spokesperson of the Union of Forest Peoples. He spoke out for the rubber-tappers and Amazonian Indians, people who rely on the forest and utilise it **sustainably** (see pages 6 and 12–13). Mendes denounced those within Brazil and abroad who either cut the forests down or provided the funding for inappropriate development projects. He was shot dead in December 1988.

One ray of hope for the world's remaining tropical rainforests is that economic arguments suggest that their destruction does not make financial sense except in the immediate short term. After only three years, the accumulated profit from the sustainable exploitation of a plot of land within the Peruvian rainforest for rubber, nuts and fruits exceeded the profit that could be gained by felling the same plot for timber.

The Convention on Biological Diversity, agreed at the 1992 Earth Summit in Rio de Janeiro, was a welcome sign. This treaty provided for countries to own the species on their land so that developing countries could derive a direct economic benefit from the exploitation of their natural resources by developed countries and multinationals. For instance, the treaty enabled tropical countries to charge royalties on medicinal products derived from their plants. However, the US refused to ratify the treaty and is still exploiting the tropics. In 1996, 750 poison arrow frogs were taken from Ecuador, apparently without permission. They were used by a pharmaceutical company in the US to develop a powerful painkiller.

While some developed northern countries demand that tropical countries implement policies that will lead to the sustainable use of their forests, the same countries refuse to be bound by such policies themselves. In Helsinki in June 1993, European governments, led by the UK, declined to commit themselves to sustainable forest exploitation. As a result this meeting, attended by 51 countries, ended in stalemate although the majority of the countries there, including the US and major tropical timber producers such as Indonesia and Malaysia, were prepared to sign. The UK refused to sign, despite the fact that Britain is one of the least wooded countries in the world. Only 8% of Britain is covered by trees, and the majority of our forests have been planted for timber, frequently with non-native species.

If the tropical forests and many other ecosystems in developing countries are to be saved, and if the whole world is not to suffer from the effects of global warming, pollution and over-fertilisation, then both developed and developing countries must learn to work together. Rich exploitative countries will have to pay for the resources they take from developing countries; they will have to stop trying to profit from Third World debts and from projects to industrialise such countries. They will have to learn how not to be rampant consumers and how to use what they have in a sustainable way. Changing lifestyles will not be easy for anyone, including those of us in the UK, but the next half-century may show whether we fail or succeed.

SAQ 6.5
Give three reasons why the primary productivity of tropical rainforests is so high.

SUMMARY

◆ Global conservation problems require international co-operation.

◆ Zoos have three main aims: conservation, education and research. Most zoos now have some captive breeding programmes as part of their conservation efforts.

◆ Captive breeding programmes usually have to be careful to avoid inbreeding depression.

◆ Botanic gardens can grow some plants and keep others in seed banks. Seed banks can also preserve the genetic diversity of crop varieties.

◆ The Convention on International Trade in Endangered Species of Wild Fauna and Flora (CITES) is an international agreement to monitor and control the trade in endangered species.

◆ The African elephant has decreased greatly in numbers since the 1960s, principally due to poaching for ivory.

◆ Saving the African elephant from extinction may involve banning trade in ivory or maximising the revenue obtained by managing elephant numbers.

◆ Tropical rainforests are the most diverse of all ecosystems. They are being cut down for a number of reasons. There are ethical and economic arguments why the tropical rainforests should be conserved.

Questions

1 Argue the case for and against there being large numbers of zoos.

2 Compare and contrast the roles that botanic gardens and zoos can play in conservation.

3 How do you feel African elephants should be conserved? Explain your reasoning.

4 Describe the significance of tropical rainforests and discuss the pressures on them.

CHAPTER 7

Ecological fieldwork

By the end of this chapter you should be able to:

1 appreciate the value of using sensors, datalogging techniques and computers when collecting and analysing ecological data;

2 measure temperature, pH, light intensity, oxygen and water content;

3 evaluate the use in different habitats of quadrats, point quadrats and belt transects for assessing species frequency, richness and percentage cover;

4 use kite diagrams to show the abundance and distribution of organisms in a belt transect;

5 assess the size of a mobile animal population using the capture–recapture technique;

6 appreciate the assumptions made in the use of the capture–recapture technique;

7 describe the properties of soil in relation to plant growth;

8 carry out a soil structure analysis;

9 use the chi-squared test, standard deviations and the t-test and assign appropriate confidence levels to experimental results.

The importance of data

Obtaining real data about organisms in their environment is the only way to test the hypotheses that ecologists and others produce and to further our understanding of a population or species. The ultimate aim may be to comprehend the workings of ecosystems, although this is certainly setting our sights high. Gathering information on living organisms in either their natural habitat ('in the field') or in laboratory and 'garden' experiments helps us with this.

Ecological fieldwork has important applied uses: for the management of endangered species, for the conservation of a habitat in a nature reserve and for the prediction of ecological problems likely during future global change. It is the basis for all the ecological and environmental theory you have read so far. Fieldwork can be a lot of fun, it can give you a feeling of satisfaction, and it can provide an insight into the workings of

the particular ecosystem you are studying which few have the privilege of achieving.

Study of an area includes observation of *biological* features, such as the presence and relative abundance of the various organisms. It also involves measurement of *physical* characteristics of the environment, such as the rainfall and temperature. Without a detailed description of the study area an ecologist will be unable to make predictions about *how* the area may change over time – whether, for example, succession will occur, or whether a particular species is at risk of dying out there.

So, in this chapter we shall look at the various techniques available to ecologists that enable them to:
■ measure aspects of the physical environment;
■ assess the relative abundance and distribution of organisms;
■ study their interrelationships.

Measuring the environment

What is the environment?

The environment of any organism is made up of the **abiotic** or **physical environment**, including such features as climate, geology and hydrology, and the **biotic environment**, which consists of other living organisms such as predators, food-stuffs, vegetation type and disease.

Much of practical ecology concentrates on terrestrial ecosystems and involves studying the physical environment, perhaps because it is easier to take definite measurements of such things as temperature and rainfall than to get to grips with several hundred species. Anyway, the physical environment affects all the species so it is a good place to start. Relevant components of the physical environment, for instance temperature and mineral levels, are called **abiotic factors**.

The vegetation in an area grows to the maximum amount allowed by the environmental conditions. Thus, if rainfall is very low, only a few specialised plants can survive and the result is desert. The higher the annual rainfall, the more lush and taller the vegetation is and the more species there usually are in the ecosystem. The hottest and wettest areas support tropical rain-forest, the most species-rich ecosystem there is

● **Figure 7.1** A whole range of measurements can be made in freshwater environments. Here two students are determining the depth of a stream.

(see page 70). Sometimes many abiotic factors operate together. For example, increased altitude is associated with a shorter growing season, greater variation in temperature, increased ultra-violet radiation and decreased partial pressures of carbon dioxide and other gases – all of which make life more difficult.

Aquatic ecosystems can be classified according to the nature of their water. How deep is it (*figure 7.1*)? Is it fresh, salty or brackish (as in an estuary)? Is the environment stable (as in deep ocean where it is always pitch dark and 4 °C) or variable (as in a sea-sonal mountain stream or tidal shore)? Are there abundant nutrients (as in a coral reef or salt marsh) or very few (as generally in deep ocean)? How much light is there? (Little light penetrates below 30 m in coastal waters and 150 m in open oceans.)

Use of datalogging techniques

Nowadays many abiotic factors can conveniently be monitored and recorded by means of **electronic sensors**. When connected to some **datalogging equipment**, such sensors allow these factors to be recorded automatically at fixed intervals over vary-ing periods of time. Such facilities are a great boon to ecologists. For instance, you could use them to record temperature, oxygen concentration and pH levels in a pond at hourly intervals over a period of 24 hours. Variation in these physical factors can then be related to variations in the physiology and behaviour of organisms, allowing testable hypotheses to be generated.

Often computer technology can be used to analyse the data obtained by using datalogging equipment. There are programs that help to create spreadsheets, draw graphs and other visual data representation and make statistical analysis a lot easier and quicker (see pages 86–90).

It should be remembered that many organisms, especially those living within other organisms or in the soil, live in microhabitats. Abiotic factors may be very different in such microhabitats compared with those in the rest of the habitat only a few millimetres away. For this reason, abiotic factors should ideally be recorded using instruments that can be positioned very precisely without affecting the microhabitat in any way. Fine, flexible probes are especially useful for this.

Measuring abiotic factors

Temperature

For poikilothermic ('cold blooded') organisms, which cannot regulate their internal temperature metabolically, the ambient temperature has a particularly significant effect on the metabolic rate and activity of the organism. Only homoiothermic ('warm blooded') birds and mammals are, to a certain extent, free from the extreme influences of temperature. Temperatures are generally best measured using electronic probes, though the traditional mercury thermometer still has value, especially if it is a maximum and minimum thermometer which displays the current temperature and records the highest and lowest temperatures experienced since it was last set.

pH

The pH of an aqueous solution is a measure of the concentration of H^+ ions dissolved in it. The higher the pH, the fewer H^+ ions there are and, in general, the more OH^- ions. On the other hand, the lower the pH, the more H^+ ions there are and the fewer the number of OH^- ions. The pH of a habitat is important, not so much because of the direct effect that H^+ or OH^- ions have on organisms, but because the pH affects the availability of other inorganic ions to these organisms. For example, at a pH below about 4.5, aluminium ions, Al^{3+}, become more soluble. This is of significance as aluminium ions are toxic to many species, particularly some plants and fish (see pages 32–33).

There are many different types of pH meter. It can be quite difficult to obtain accurate, repeatable readings. pH electrodes usually require calibration before use, in solutions of known pH, and should be treated carefully and in accordance with the manufacturer's instructions. Soil samples may require specialised preparation before their pH can be recorded. The use of universal indicator solution, which changes colour depending on whether the soil is acidic (red) or alkaline (blue), is the simplest way to compare the pH of soils.

Light levels

Light intensity and wavelength are of great importance to organisms, particularly those that photosynthesise. Specialised equipment is needed to record the **spectral composition** of light, that is the relative contribution of different wavelengths. Blue and red light are absorbed and used more than green light by chloroplasts, which is why most leaves are green in colour. Blue light, being of a shorter wavelength, penetrates water more than green or red. Because of this, many seaweeds have pigments that trap only these shorter wavelengths. As a result, such seaweeds are brown or red in colour.

Several types of **light meter** are available and the details of their operation need not concern us. Various units are used when recording **light intensity**. Perhaps the most widely used unit is watts per square metre ($W\,m^{-2}$), used to measure the total radiation falling on an area. Other instruments record the **intensity of visible radiation** falling on an area (measured in lux) and still others record the **intensity of photosynthetically active radiation** (also measured in lux). The important thing is to use the same instrument in the same way when taking a number of readings.

Oxygen content

Atmospheric oxygen concentrations vary little, but in water and soil, oxygen concentrations can vary greatly. It is difficult to determine the oxygen content of the air in soil, as the sampling method tends to introduce atmospheric air. However, the oxygen content of water can be measured either by the use of probes within the natural habitat or by determining the oxygen content of a sample taken underwater so as not to introduce air bubbles.

The traditional method is the **Winkler technique**. A sample of water is obtained and the oxygen content determined by a chemical method in which the manganese ion Mn^{2+} is oxidised to Mn^{3+}. The amount of Mn^{3+} is then determined by titration. The Winkler technique is reliable but fiddly and difficult to carry out in the field. (It requires a number of different chemical reagents, including concentrated sulphuric acid.) Nowadays probes are more often used. Within the probe a current is generated, the size of which depends on the dissolved oxygen content. Oxygen probes can be temperamental and careful calibration is always advisable.

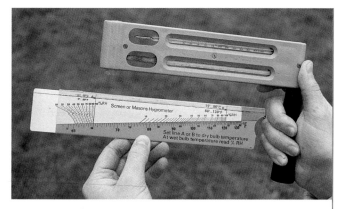

● **Figure 7.2** A wet and dry bulb hygrometer, used to measure relative humidity.

Water content

Water is a major constituent of living cells and necessary for metabolism. Obtaining and keeping water is vital for most organisms. Atmospheric humidity is an important factor affecting many organisms. **Relative humidity** is the most frequently used expression of the amount of water in the air. It is the percentage of water vapour the air holds relative to that which it would hold if it were fully saturated. It can be measured by means of a **wet and dry bulb hygrometer** (*figure 7.2*). However, it is difficult to measure the relative humidity of microhabitats. Determination of soil water content is described on page 85.

Mineral content

Levels of nitrate (NO_3^-), phosphate (PO_4^{3-}), potassium (K^+) and a number of other mineral ions are of great importance to plants and other organisms in soil and water. Unfortunately, accurate measurements of most minerals are difficult, especially in soils. Various kits can be obtained from garden centres, aquarium suppliers and specialised sources, and some electronic probes are also available. Whilst the absolute levels recorded by some of the kits may be imprecise, valid comparisons between different habitats can generally be made.

Measuring populations

Population biology

A population was defined in chapter 1 as a group of individuals of one species with the opportunity to breed with one another because they live in the same area. In reality, however, it is extremely difficult in natural situations to tell how large a population actually is, or exactly which individuals belong to it. Often all the organisms of one species in an area are assumed to be in the same population if the area is a 'reasonable' size. It is, of course, glaringly obvious that plants are different from animals. Plants are stationary so they are easy to count, but they often increase by vegetative growth so it may be difficult to recognise individuals. (How many individual grasses are in a lawn?) Animal individuals are usually easy to recognise but highly mobile, so difficult to count. Many seashore animals, including barnacles, sea anemones and molluscs, are sessile or slow enough for counting to be easy and can be recorded in the same way as plants (see page 79). .

When studying a population you can go in at one point in time and look at all the individuals alive at that moment to determine their ages, health and so on. Another approach is to look at all the individuals born in one year (or day, depending on the lifespan of the organisms) and follow that **cohort**, seeing what is the fate of each individual. This, of course, may be a problem if the lifespan of the species is hundreds of years! Sometimes a cohort from the past can be 'followed' if the organisms can be aged.

Trees growing outside the tropics can be accurately aged as they have annual growth rings in their wood, and some animals can be aged using growth rings on scales, shells, teeth or the small bones in the inner ear. A core from a tree or a single scale from a fish can be removed without much harm to the organism, but other methods may require the animal to have died. Many ecological studies of the past have relied on collecting specimens or have caused the death of organisms. One classic experiment required the fumigation of a series of islands to study re-colonisation. Obviously very careful thought and justification is required before any decision is made to harm the organisms in the ecosystem being studied.

Instead of choosing to investigate the population dynamics of a single species, an alternative approach is to study the whole community. The first problem is the identification of all the species. For a well-known area such as Europe, there are many books containing photographs, drawings and **identification keys** that can be used to identify the genera and species present. Identification keys ask a series of questions about the morphology of the organism and by following the questions through, the answers (hopefully) lead to the correct species. They can be quite difficult to use but usually the features that have to be noted are well explained and illustrated at the beginning of each key.

There is a problem in less well-studied areas, such as tropical forest, where not only are there fewer if any useful books, but also many of the species may not yet have been identified and named. This is less of a problem with plants, most of which *have* been identified to species level, but is definitely the case for insects.

The simplest record of a community is how many species it contains: the **species richness**. Species richness could be represented by a single number, the number of species in total in the described community, but it is much more meaningful when the species are classified into **taxonomic groups**. Species could be grouped as plants, animals, fungi and bacteria, or in more detail as mammals, fish, insects, spiders and so on. A single number will not tell you very much, but the more detailed taxonomic groupings will give an idea of the type of ecosystem being studied and even something about the food webs in the system.

Species richness is part of the whole concept of biodiversity. The widest understanding of the **biodiversity** of an ecosystem includes the number of species, but it also includes the taxonomic diversity of the species, the number and distribution of individuals in populations and even the genetic diversity within the populations, as well as a feel for the stability of the ecosystem. Quite often when you read about global biodiversity, the writer is mainly referring to species richness. This is because species richness is often the only measure we have, but it is at least a good indication of the underlying more complex biodiversity.

Measuring plants and stationary animals

Because of the uneven distribution of organisms in most environments, ecologists need to employ **random sampling** to determine the abundance of individuals. Random sampling prevents you choosing to put the quadrat down over some pretty flowers or over a bare area if you want to reduce your effort! Suppose you are studying the plants in a meadow 40 m long and 15 m wide. You will need a table of random numbers which lie evenly between 0 and 10, or some other device, such as a computer program, to give you these numbers. (Tables of random numbers are included in most statistical tables.) Now obtain one random number between 0 and 10. Multiply it by 4. This tells you how far to go in metres along the longer side of the meadow. Now obtain a second random number between 0 and 10 and multiply it by 1.5 (because the meadow is 15 m wide). This tells you how far to go in metres along the shorter side of the meadow. You now have two co-ordinates to tell you where to place a quadrat. Repeat this process with more numbers from the random number table until you have put the quadrat down in quite a few places. The number of quadrats to take is always a balance between time and accuracy. The more quadrats you record, the more representative your results will be but also the longer it will take.

Quadrats

A **quadrat** is a sampling unit of a known area. Quadrats are usually square frames that can be carried about and positioned with ease (e.g. *figure 7.3*). The size of the quadrat depends on the

● **Figure 7.3** A quadrat in use on a rocky sea-shore.

habitat and the organisms to be examined. Plant quadrats are often 0.5 m × 0.5 m. This size is ideal for grassland. Larger quadrats may be needed for heathland or woodland. This is because too small a quadrat may lead, by chance, to one species (e.g. an oak tree) being over-represented or under-represented. Anyway, you try getting a 0.5 m^2 quadrat over an oak tree! There are no hard and fast rules but quadrats of up to 4 m × 4 m may be needed in woodland. Of course, the disadvantage with such a large quadrat is that it takes a long time to use. There is therefore a trade-off between the advantage of using a larger quadrat (more data obtained) and the disadvantage (more time taken). You could, of course, use a small quadrat to sample the ground flora of the wood and a very large one to sample the tree species.

In general the more quadrats taken in an area, the better the results will be. In species-poor or uniform habitats a small number of quadrats will be sufficient. In species-rich or heterogenous habitats a hundred quadrats or more may be required. A possible 'rule of thumb' to use is to plot cumulative number of species (y-axis) against number of quadrats already taken (x-axis). When the curve levels off, that is a suitable number of quadrats to have taken.

In much the same way, the optimal quadrat size for a habitat can be determined by calculating the mean number of species per quadrat for a range of quadrats of different sizes. When the mean number of species per quadrat (y-axis) is plotted against quadrat area (x-axis), the optimal quadrat size is indicated by the point at which the curve levels off.

Quadrats can be used to measure the abundance of any sessile organism: plants, lichens, attached seaweeds, limpets, barnacles and other seashore invertebrates. The simplest measure is **species frequency**. Each species is recorded as present or absent in each quadrat. The species frequency equals the percentage of quadrats in which the species is found. For example, suppose you examine ten quadrats in an oak woodland and find that bluebells are present in three of them. Bluebells are said to occur with a frequency of 30%. Note that this figure depends on the size of the quadrat so it is a good idea always to say how large your quadrat was.

Quadrats can also be used to measure the **density** of individuals. The density of the individuals in a species is the average number of individuals of that species found per unit area. So, for example, if ten 0.5 m × 0.5 m quadrats reveal a total of 140 bluebells in an oak woodland, the density is given by:

$$\text{density} = \text{number of individuals} \div \text{area}$$
$$= 140 \div (10 \times 0.5\,\text{m} \times 0.5\,\text{m})$$
$$= 140 \div 2.5\,\text{m}^2$$
$$= 56\,\text{m}^{-2}$$

i.e. 56 bluebells per square metre.

The major problem with using density as a measure of the abundance of some species is knowing where one individual ends and another one of the same species begins. This is not usually a problem when studying animals but with many plants which put out runners, root suckers or rhizomes it can be impossible to decide where one individual finishes and another starts.

Because of the difficulties of using species density as a measure of abundance, another approach is to determine **percentage cover**. Here the percentage of each quadrat covered by each species is measured. The percentage can either be recorded as a number (e.g. 1% or 15%) or a scale can be used. One widely used scale is the **DAFOR scale**. D stands for dominant, A for abundant, F for frequent, O for occasional and R for rare. Another, the **ACFOR scale** (Abundant, Common, Frequent, Occasional, Rare), is sometimes considered better as it is unusual for a single species to be dominant in a quadrat or habitat. Obviously these scales are subjective so it is difficult to get consistent agreement between different people – in other words, inter-observer

Cover (%)	Braun-Blanquet scale
< 1	+
1–5	1
6–25	2
26–50	3
51–75	4
76–100	5

● **Table 7.1** The Braun-Blanquet scale used to assess the percentage cover of vegetation.

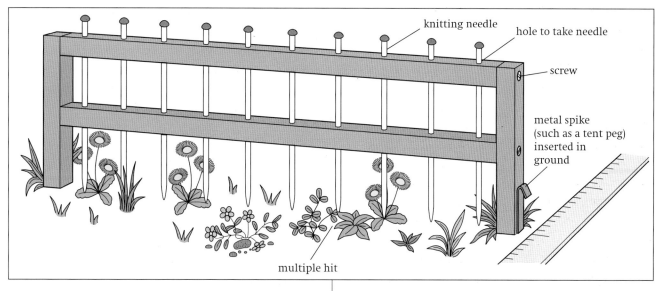

knitting needle

hole to take needle

screw

metal spike (such as a tent peg) inserted in ground

multiple hit

● **Figure 7.4** A home-made point quadrat frame with all ten needles lowered onto the vegetation.

reliability is low. However, they are quick and useful when employed by one person working alone with a large number of quadrats to assess.

A more objective scale for assessing the percentage cover of vegetation is the **Braun-Blanquet scale**, explained in *table 7.1*. Whatever the method used to estimate percentage cover, the accuracy can often be improved by subdividing the quadrat. For instance, pieces of string can be placed at 10 cm intervals to divide a 0.5 m × 0.5 m quadrat into 25 smaller quadrats.

Another type of quadrat is the **point quadrat** (*figure 7.4*). Imagine you are assessing the abundance of plant species in a habitat using species frequency (i.e. the percentage of the quadrats in which the species occur). Now imagine that the quadrat size gets smaller and smaller, ending up as a point. In this case, placing a quadrat on the vegetation is equivalent to placing a needle, or point, on the vegetation. This is what a point quadrat is. All you need to do is to record the percentage of the needles (i.e. point quadrats) that come into contact with each species as each needle is lowered vertically. Note that it is perfectly possible for one needle to strike more than one species, so that the total of all the percentages determined by point quadrats may exceed 100%. Point quadrats are most often used when the vegetation is low in height and dense.

SAQ 7.1

What is the frequency of daisies (expressed as a percentage) in *figure 7.4*?

Investigating the distribution of species

The distribution of immobile species can be studied using **transects**. 'Transect' means 'cut across' and transects are of two types. A **line transect** is when a long piece of string or rope is placed on the ground and the organisms in contact with the line are identified and their position along the line recorded. A **belt transect** is when a series of quadrats is placed along a line at regular intervals and the organisms in each quadrat identified and their abundance recorded.

Transects are particularly useful when a clear change in the species of organisms occurs between the two ends of the transect. For example, transects can be used to investigate the changes in vegetation as you go from grassland into neighbouring woodland, or the changes in sessile animals (barnacles, limpets, periwinkles, etc.) as you go up a rocky shore from the sea to the high tide zone and beyond, or changes in vegetation as you climb a mountain.

The data obtained from a belt transect can be represented on **kite diagrams** (*figure 7.5*), where the width of the 'kite' shape represents the abundance of the organism at that point, and the overall shape of the kite shows the distribution of the organism along the transect. Kite diagrams are often used by

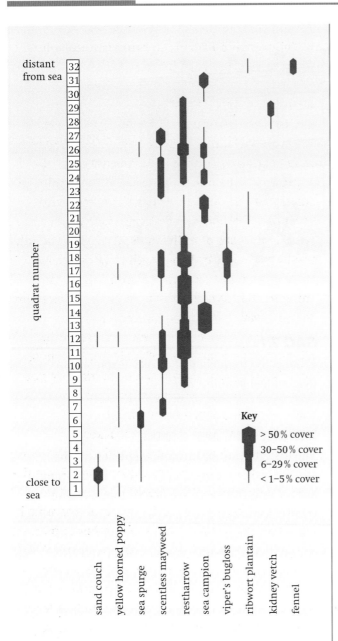

distant from sea

quadrat number

close to sea

Key

> 50 % cover

30–50 % cover

6–29 % cover

< 1–5 % cover

sand couch
yellow horned poppy
sea spurge
scentless mayweed
restharrow
sea campion
viper's bugloss
ribwort plantain
kidney vetch
fennel

● **Figure 7.5** A kite diagram of data collected by students on a belt transect of Slapton Shingle Bank in Devon from the storm ridge close to the sea (early succession and disturbed) to the roadside (later succession and less disturbed). The 1 m^2 quadrats are numbered up the left-hand side.

palaeontologists to show the changing abundance of organisms through evolutionary time.

SAQ 7.2

What effect would taking the same number of quadrats, but increasing the size of the quadrat used, have on the measured species frequency?

● **Figure 7.6** A Longworth trap used to catch small mammals such as voles and mice.

Catching mobile animals

Various techniques are available to study the distribution of mobile organisms. **Longworth traps** are designed to catch small mammals without harming them. They are usually baited with sufficient food to keep the trapped animal well fed (*figure 7.6*). If set out at regular intervals on a grid, these traps can be used to map the distribution of small mammals such as mice and voles. In much the same way, the distribution of ground arthropods can be studied using **pitfall traps** (*figure 7.7*). Insects and other arthropods on plants can be collected by the use of strong **nets** or **beating trays**. A **pooter** (*figure 7.8*) can then be used to gather specimens for

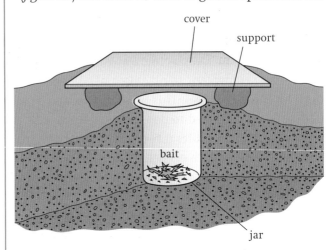

cover

support

bait

jar

● **Figure 7.7** A pitfall trap complete with bait. The cover excludes rain and certain predators.

● **Figure 7.8** Dr Nigel Franks using a pooter to capture ants. His research on ant behaviour in colonies is intended to help roboticists and computer scientists design better machines.

identification, after which the organisms can be returned to their natural habitat.

Freshwater organisms can be sampled using nets. Coarse nets have a mesh of about 1 mm and gather larger invertebrates and fish. Finer nets will also sample **plankton** – small aquatic organisms that drift almost passively. A mesh size of 0.3 mm is suitable for **zooplankton** (the larvae of animals) and a mesh size of 0.075 mm (75 μm) can be used for **phytoplankton** (e.g. microscopic algae) and protozoa (unicellular heterotrophs such as *Amoeba* and *Paramecium*).

One way of sampling freshwater invertebrates in a stream or river is by **kick sampling**. This method is particularly suitable for animals that live in or on the bed of a stream. A coarse net is held downstream of the area to be sampled. The bed of the stream immediately upstream of the net is then disturbed by three or four kicks directed upstream. Dislodged animals are carried into the net by the current. Although the method may sound crude, if consistently applied in different areas it can allow semi-quantitative comparisons to be made. It is advisable to wear Wellington boots.

Other sampling approaches to examine the distribution of organisms include:
- mist nets to catch birds or bats which can then be given identification rings (but only licensed and trained people are allowed to catch, handle and ring such animals);
- light traps to catch night-flying moths;
- **Tullgren** and **Baermann funnels** to sample soil organisms (see page 86).

The capture–recapture technique

The **capture–recapture** technique can be used to calculate the abundance (or population size) of mobile animals. Indeed it actually requires the organisms to be mobile to get accurate results. In this technique, also known as the **mark–release–recapture** method, the first stage is to catch a reasonable number of individuals. Voles, for example, might be caught by Longworth traps (*figure 7.6*).

Having caught a sample of animals, the next thing to do is to count them and then mark them in some way that causes neither harm nor distress. Voles, for instance, can be marked by clipping off a small piece of their fur. Whirligig beetles (an aquatic insect) can be marked by putting a tiny drop of waterproof paint on one of their elytra (hardened front wings).

After the animals have been marked satisfactorily, they are released and allowed to mix thoroughly with the rest of the unmarked population. This is where their mobility is important. After a suitable period of time, a second sample is obtained and counted, and the number of marked individuals recorded. An estimate of the total size of the population can then be made. Suppose you mark 30 whirligig beetles and then release them back into their original habitat – a ditch. A few hours later, once the marked individuals have mixed with the rest of the population, you catch 40 whirligig beetles from the same area and find that five of them are marked. As only one in eight (i.e. 5 out of 40) of the animals you caught the second time were marked, the chances are that you only marked one-eighth of the total population. In that case, the best estimate you can make of the overall population size is 30 × 8, i.e. 240.

The equation for working out an estimate of the size of a population by this method is called the **Lincoln index**. It is given by the formula:

$$\text{population size} = \frac{n_1 \times n_2}{n_m}$$

where n_1 is the number of individuals marked and released ('1' because it was the first sample),

n_2 is the number of individuals caught the second time round ('2' because it was the second sample) and n_m is the number of marked individuals in the second sample ('m' standing for marked).

So your estimate for the whirligig beetles would be $\dfrac{30 \times 40}{5} = 240$

Using the Lincoln index to estimate population size involves making a number of assumptions:

■ the marked animals mix thoroughly back into the original population;

■ marked and unmarked animals do not differ in any significant way – for example, marked individuals are no more likely to emigrate from the population or die than are unmarked individuals;

■ the marks do not wear off before the second sample is taken;

■ no (or very few) births or immigrations into the population occur between the first release of the marked animals and the capture of the second set of animals.

SAQ 7.3

Suppose that in a mark–release–recapture exercise, 83 woodmice are initially captured and marked and 127 subsequently recaptured, of which 23 carry the mark. To the nearest 10 animals, calculate the best estimate for the number of woodmice in the population.

SAQ 7.4

Predict the effect on the estimate of population size using the Lincoln index in each of the following circumstances:

(i) Insufficient time elapses before the animals are recaptured, and the second sample is taken from the same place as the first;

(ii) Insufficient time elapses before the animals are recaptured, and the second sample is taken from a different place to the first;

(iii) Some of the marks wear off before the second sample is taken;

(iv) Marked animals are more likely to be caught by predators;

(v) Marked animals become 'trap-happy' and are more likely to be caught in traps (e.g. because traps are baited with food);

(vi) The interval between the first and second sample is such that most of the individuals in the original population have died and been replaced by new births.

Soils

Soil structure

Soil is composed of inorganic (mineral) particles and organic matter together with water and air. The inorganic matter in soil comes from the erosion of rocks in the area, often called the bedrock. Rocks have been weathered and eroded for millions of years so the accumulation of soil, especially in hollows and valleys, can be very deep. Soil on hillsides tends to be shallower because much of it is washed down by rain and carried away in streams. Sandstone rocks weather to produce sandy soils whereas granites usually release clays. Limestone tends to dissolve in the slightly acidic rain (see page 31) and hardly produces any soil, so soils over limestone tend to be very shallow.

Soil particle size can be important for soil structure and hence plant growth: a soil with mostly very small clay particles (table 7.2) is heavy. It can be waterlogged when wet or baked hard when dry. A soil with a high sand content is a lighter soil, which is much more easily drained and soon dries out. Particle sizes between clay and sand are called silt (table 7.2). If the water content of a soil falls during a period of drought, plants growing in it may wilt or even die unless they have very deep roots that reach down to a remaining water supply. If the water content increases during prolonged heavy rain or flooding, this drives the air out of the soil and waterlogging results, which can kill roots and soil animals.

Particle type	Particle diameter
clay	$<2\,\mu m$
silt	$2\text{–}20\,\mu m$
fine sand	$20\text{–}200\,\mu m$
sand	$200\,\mu m\text{–}2\,mm$
gravel	$>2\,mm$

● Table 7.2 Soil particle size classes.

Organic matter in soils comes from the decaying material of plants (leaves, twigs and roots) and animals (insect remains, for example). Soil also contains many living organisms: roots, worms, collembola (springtails), nematodes, bacteria, fungi and even a few mammals such as gophers and badgers.

If you dig a trench you will see the soil has a layered structure (*figure 7.9*). The topmost layer is loosely packed and high in organic matter especially in temperate regions in autumn, when the leaves have just fallen. This is the **litter layer**. Once the litter is decomposed by soil organisms it becomes very dark – almost black – and forms the humic layer underneath the litter. The decaying **humus** releases mineral nutrients such as nitrate, phosphate and potassium ions. Soils also contain many heavy metal ions in very low concentrations. These are known as **trace elements** and are required in small amounts by plants and animals for healthy growth. It is only when heavy metal ions get into surface soils in high concentrations that they become toxic to organisms (see page 30). As you dig deeper, you will find layers with less humus (washed down or leached from above) and more clay, silt or sand – this is the **topsoil**. Humus is still present in deeper soil and helps give it its structure, water-retaining capacity and fertility. If you dig very deep you dig through the **subsoil** and will eventually get to parent material and bedrock.

Analysis of soils

Soil can be analysed to determine the proportions of the different components: organic matter (the litter and humus content), soil particle sizes, water and air. The pH of a soil can also be measured (see page 77).

The **litter content** can be determined by mixing a sample of the surface layers of soil with a large amount of water. The organic matter will float while the mineral particles sink – sand rapidly and clay very slowly. You will probably have to rescue several animals that are also floating in the litter. The litter can then be removed and picked over to identify the fragments. The **humus content** is too dispersed to float off like this and the best way to determine it is to weigh a dry sample of soil, crush it, then heat it to a high temperature to burn off all

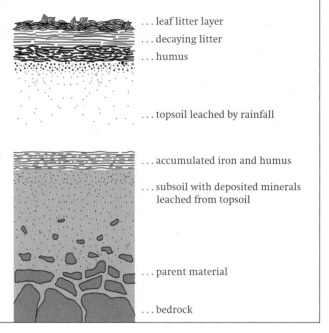

... leaf litter layer

... decaying litter

... humus

... topsoil leached by rainfall

... accumulated iron and humus

... subsoil with deposited minerals leached from topsoil

... parent material

... bedrock

● **Figure 7.9** A typical soil profile showing the layered structure.

the organic matter and weigh it again. Then:

humus mass = initial dry mass – final dry mass

SAQ 7.5

After carrying out the above procedure to determine the humus content of a soil, what is left in the sample?

Particle size can initially be assessed by rubbing a small lump of wet soil between the finger and thumb: a slippery, sticky soil has a high clay content; a gritty soil a high sand content. To determine particle size more accurately requires sieving dried and crushed soil through a set of **soil sieves** with different sized meshes to collect first gravel, then sand, then silt and finally clay. Care needs to be taken not to inhale the dusty clay, which is bad for the lungs.

The **amount of water in a soil** can be determined as follows:
1 weigh a sample of the soil ($M_{initial}$);
2 heat the soil at 105 °C until a constant mass is attained (M_{final}); 24 hours is generally long enough;
3 the percentage of water in the original soil is given by:

$$\% \text{ water} = \frac{M_{initial} - M_{final}}{M_{initial}} \times 100$$

For **air content**, take a known volume of undisturbed soil gathered carefully with some sort of borer and placed so it fits snugly in a container of the same shape and size. Then add water from a measuring cylinder. The volume of water taken up to just saturate the soil is equivalent to the volume of air in the pore spaces.

Determining the **nutrient content** of soils or any other sample (such as leaves) is notoriously unreliable (see page 78). Kits can be obtained to analyse the nitrate, phosphate and calcium content, but if you get very interested in soils you could probably devise some plant growth experiments in untreated soils and soils with known added nutrients to compare growth.

Some of the **organisms** living in the soil can be retrieved during litter separation or can be hand picked (or chased) out of litter samples. Other extraction methods use **Tullgren funnels**, which catch air-dwelling organisms from dry soil, or **Baermann funnels** which collect organisms from the water layers in the pore spaces (*figure 7.10*). In both cases, the principle is that organisms move down away from a source of light and heat and are caught.

Many of these soil organisms will be killed during extraction, so thought is needed as to how many samples are necessary for study. You may get more fun by actually keeping soil organisms and studying their behaviour. Earthworms and associated invertebrates can be kept in a wormery with glass sides so the activity of the animals can be watched.

Analysing data

The chi-squared test

The chi-squared test (also known as the χ^2 test since the Greek letter 'χ' is pronounced 'chi') allows you to compare sets of data you have collected to see whether the ratios or proportions of your results are as expected (see *Biology 2*, chapter 4). For example, does the proportion of plant species that are woody differ between two ecosystems? The chi-squared test can only be carried out on *whole* numbers that vary *discontinuously*. This means that the chi-squared test is normally only used if you have counted, for example, distinct individuals or the number of quadrats in which a species occurs. It cannot, for instance, be used if the units of what you have measured are those of time (e.g. seconds or hours) or distance, nor can it be used on percentages.

An example will help illustrate how to carry out a chi-squared test. (You are most likely to design an experiment where you take equal numbers of quadrats from each habitat but, if for any reason you don't, the test is perfectly valid even when there are different numbers of quadrats taken in the habitats you are comparing. The example given here, therefore, uses different quadrat numbers so

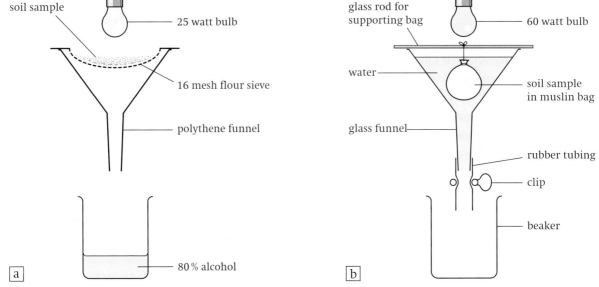

● **Figure 7.10 a** Home-made Tullgren funnel for collecting air-dwelling organisms from dry soil.
  b Home-made Baermann funnel for collecting organisms living in soil pore water layers.

you can see how such calculations proceed. Note the quadrats *do* have to be the same size.) Suppose in an ecological study you look at fifty 0.5 m × 0.5 m quadrats in one wood (wood A) and one hundred 0.5 m × 0.5 m quadrats in another wood (wood B). You then look at how many of these quadrats contain grass. You find that 30 of the quadrats in wood A contain grass compared to 25 of the quadrats in wood B. The question is, does the proportion of the quadrats that contain grass differ significantly between the two woods?

We can see that 30 out of 50 of the quadrats in wood A contain grass compared to only 25 out of 100 in wood B. It looks as though the two woods do indeed differ in the proportion of the quadrats that contain grass. But how sure are we of this conclusion? Perhaps the differences are due only to chance. Traditionally, statisticians only like to draw conclusions about differences between samples if they are 95% sure that these differences are real. So we should only conclude that the woods differ in the proportions of their quadrats that contain grass if we are 95% sure of this.

The first thing to do is to work out the expected numbers of quadrats in each of the two woods that would contain grass *on the null hypothesis that any differences between the woods are simply due to chance.* Given this null hypothesis, we can say that as the 150 quadrats have between them 55 (i.e. 30 + 25) quadrats with grass, the chance of any one quadrat containing grass is 55 ÷ 150 = 0.367. We would therefore, if our null hypothesis is correct, expect that in wood A 50 × 0.367 = 18.3 of the quadrats should contain grass while in wood B 100 × 0.367 = 36.7 should. It may look odd expecting non-whole numbers, but this is the only way to get the same proportion (0.367) of the quadrats in each wood containing grass.

Now complete the following table:

	Wood A	Wood B
observed (O)	30	25
expected (E)	18.3	36.7
O − E	11.7	−11.7
$(O - E)^2$	136.9	136.9
$(O - E)^2 \div E$	7.5	3.7
sum of $\{(O - E)^2 \div E\}$ = 7.5 + 3.7 = 11.2		

Degrees of freedom	Value of chi-squared			
1	2.71	3.84	6.64	10.8
2	4.61	5.99	9.21	13.8
3	6.25	7.82	11.3	16.3
4	7.78	9.49	13.3	18.5
Probability that chance could have produced this value of chi-squared	0.10	0.05	0.01	0.001
Confidence level	10%	5%	1%	0.1%

● **Table 7.3** Table of chi-squared values.

Here, 11.2 is called the **chi-squared value**. The bigger it is, the greater the chance that the observed results differ significantly from the expected ones. To see if the difference is significant, use *table 7.3*. Note that you need to know the **degrees of freedom**. For a chi-squared test, the degrees of freedom are simply one less than the number of classes of data. In our example, the number of classes of data equals two, because each quadrat either contained grass or did not – i.e. there were just two possibilities.

If the value of chi-squared is bigger than the critical value – the one that corresponds to a 5% probability that chance could have produced it – in *table 7.3*, we can be at least 95% confident that the difference between the observed and expected results is significant. The result is said to be **statistically significant** at the 5% **confidence level**.

You can see that in our example, the value of chi-squared we calculated (11.2) is much bigger than the critical value (3.84). This means that the two woods differ very significantly in the proportion of their quadrats that contain grass. Had our value of chi-squared been between 3.84 and 6.64 we would have been between 95% and 99% certain that the difference between the observed and expected results is significant. Similarly, had it been between 6.64 and 10.8 we would have been between 99% and 99.9% certain that the difference between the observed and expected results is significant. As our value exceeds 10.8, we are at least 99.9% certain that the two types of woods differ in the proportion of their quadrats that contain grass. *The difference between the two types of wood is statistically significant at the 0.1% confidence level.*

The general formula you need to carry out a chi-squared test is:

$$\text{chi-squared} = \Sigma \frac{(O - E)^2}{E}$$

where Σ means 'sum of'. The degrees of freedom are equal to one less than the number of classes. As always in statistics, the more data the better. For technical reasons a chi-squared test should have each expected value, E, equal to 5 or more.

The t-test

The **t-test** allows you to see whether the means of two sets of data differ significantly. Here is a hypothetical example to illustrate how it works. Suppose you measure the number of species of lichen found in eight urban churchyards and six rural churchyards within 10 km of your school or college. You end up with 14 bits of data, as follows:

> number of lichen species in urban churchyards: 6, 4, 6, 5, 3, 7, 5, 3
> number of lichen species in rural churchyards: 6, 6, 8, 5, 9, 7

It looks as though there may be more species of lichen in the rural churchyards but it is difficult to be sure of this simply by looking at the data. How can we investigate this statistically? The first thing to do is to calculate the **means**.

Calculating means
You will have calculated means before. All you have to do is to add up the individual values and divide by the total number of measurements. So, in this case, the mean number of lichen species in the urban churchyards is:

$$(6 + 4 + 6 + 5 + 3 + 7 + 5 + 3) \div 8 = 4.875$$

The general formula is:

$$\bar{x} = \Sigma x/n$$

where:

> $\bar{x}$ is the mean
> Σ stands for 'sum of'
> x refers to the individual values in the sample
> n is the total number of individual values in the sample.

Repeating this exercise with the rural lichens, we find that their mean number is 6.833. The next thing we need to do is to calculate **standard deviations**. The standard deviation is a measure of the extent to which individual measurements *vary* around the mean. The greater the variation among the individual measurements, the bigger the standard deviation; the less the variation among the individual measurements, the smaller the standard deviation.

It helps to have a calculator that works out standard deviations. If you *don't* have such a calculator, read the next section, entitled 'Calculating standard deviations'. If you *do* have a calculator that works out standard deviations, you may want to skip this section and go to the section entitled 'Using a calculator to obtain standard deviations'.

Calculating standard deviations
The standard deviation, s_x, is given by the following formula:

$$s_x = \sqrt{\frac{\Sigma x^2 - \frac{(\Sigma x)^2}{n}}{n - 1}}$$

where:

> Σ stands for 'sum of'
> x refers to the individual values in the sample
> n is the total number of individual values in the sample.

In the case of our eight urban lichens, the eight individual values, i.e. values of x, are: 6, 4, 6, 5, 3, 7, 5 and 3. The sum of these eight values, i.e. Σx, equals 39. (You can forget about any units while actually doing the calculations provided you put them in at the end – the mean and the standard deviation have the same units as the individual values of x.) Using these values of x and Σx in the above formula, we have:

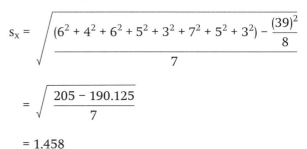

$$s_x = \sqrt{\frac{(6^2 + 4^2 + 6^2 + 5^2 + 3^2 + 7^2 + 5^2 + 3^2) - \frac{(39)^2}{8}}{7}}$$

$$= \sqrt{\frac{205 - 190.125}{7}}$$

$$= 1.458$$

Using a calculator to obtain standard deviations

You may need to have your calculator in standard deviation mode, and type the data into a memory. Then there will be a key, often labelled x. This key gives you the mean of the data. Another key, often labelled s or σ, gives you the standard deviation. If you have the key σ_{n-1} or s_{n-1} use it in preference to σ_n or s_n for working out the standard deviation.

Using standard deviations to calculate the significance of the difference between two means

If you have a decidedly up-market calculator (or access to a statistical computer package) you may have a key labelled t. This stands for **t-test** because that is the name of the test we are going to carry out. If you do have such a key, use it as instructed by the calculator or statistical package and go to step 8 below. If you don't have a key labelled t, proceed as follows:

1 Work out the means of the two sets of data.
2 Subtract the smaller mean from the larger one.
3 Work out the standard deviation of one set of data. Multiply this number by itself (i.e. square it) and divide it by the number of pieces of data in that set of data.
4 Work out the standard deviation of the other set of data. Multiply this number by itself (i.e. square it) and divide it by the number of pieces of data in that set of data.
5 Add together the figures you calculated in steps 3 and 4.
6 Take the square root of the figure calculated in step 5.
7 Divide the difference between the two means (step 2) by the figure calculated in step 6. This is your t value.
8 Now use *table 7.4* to see whether your value of t could be expected by chance. For a t-test, the degrees of freedom are simply two less than the total number of individual measurements in the two samples.

■ If your value of t is bigger than the critical value – the one that corresponds to a 5% probability that chance could have produced it – in *table 7.4* you can be at least 95% confident that the difference between the means is significant. Your result is said to be statistically significant and you can reject the null hypothesis that there is no difference between the means.

■ If your value of t is smaller than the critical value in *table 7.4* you are less than 95% confident that the difference between the means is significant. Your result is not statistically

Degrees of freedom	Value of t			
1	6.31	12.7	63.7	636
2	2.92	4.30	9.93	31.6
3	2.35	3.18	5.84	12.9
4	2.13	2.78	4.60	8.61
5	2.02	2.57	4.03	6.87
6	1.94	2.45	3.71	5.96
7	1.90	2.37	3.50	5.41
8	1.86	2.31	3.36	5.04
9	1.83	2.26	3.25	4.78
10	1.81	2.23	3.17	4.59
11	1.80	2.20	3.11	4.44
12	1.78	2.18	3.06	4.32
13	1.77	2.16	3.01	4.22
14	1.76	2.15	2.98	4.14
15	1.75	2.13	2.95	4.07
16	1.75	2.12	2.92	4.02
17	1.74	2.11	2.90	3.97
18	1.73	2.10	2.88	3.92
19	1.73	2.09	2.86	3.88
20	1.73	2.09	2.85	3.85
22	1.72	2.07	2.82	3.79
24	1.71	2.06	2.80	3.75
26	1.71	2.06	2.78	3.71
28	1.70	2.05	2.76	3.67
30	1.70	2.04	2.75	3.65
40	1.68	2.02	2.70	3.55
50	1.68	2.01	2.70	3.52
60	1.67	2.00	2.66	3.46
70	1.67	1.99	2.65	3.44
80	1.66	1.99	2.64	3.42
90	1.66	1.99	2.63	3.40
100	1.66	1.99	2.63	3.39
Probability that chance could have produced this value of t	0.10	0.05	0.01	0.001
Confidence level	10%	5%	1%	0.1%

● **Table 7.4** Table of t values.

significant and you cannot reject the null hypothesis that there is no difference between the means.

To help make this easier to understand here's a worked example using our data on the number of lichen species in rural and urban churchyards.

1 Mean number of urban lichen species = 4.875; mean number of rural lichen species = 6.833.

2 Difference between the means = 1.958.

3 Standard deviation of the number of urban lichens multiplied by itself divided by the number of pieces of data in that set of data = $1.458 \times 1.458 \div 8 = 0.266$.

4 Standard deviation of the number of rural lichens multiplied by itself divided by the number of pieces of data in that set of data = $1.472 \times 1.472 \div 6 = 0.361$.

5 The sum of the figures calculated in steps 3 and 4 = 0.266 + 0.361 = 0.627.

6 The square root of the figure calculated in step 5 = 0.792.

7 The difference between the two means (step 2) divided by the figure calculated in step 6 = 1.958 ÷ 0.792 = 2.47.

8 It is clear that 2.47 is greater than the critical value of t, which for a total of 12 degrees of freedom equals 2.18. This means that we are at least 95% confident that the mean number of

lichens differs between urban and rural church-yards. Note that our value of t would have had to have been equal to at least 3.06 for us to have been 99% confident of this conclusion.

We can sum up the way to calculate the value of t by these steps as follows:

$$t = \frac{\bar{x} - \bar{y}}{\sqrt{\dfrac{(s_x)^2}{n_x} + \dfrac{(s_y)^2}{n_y}}}$$

where:

$\bar{x}$ equals the mean of sample X
$\bar{y}$ equals the mean of sample Y
s_x is the standard deviation of sample X
s_y is the standard deviation of sample Y
n_x is the number of individual measurements in sample X
n_y is the number of individual measurements in sample Y.

The degrees of freedom are equal to $n_x + n_y - 2$.

One final point. The larger your sample sizes, the more likely you are to detect a significant difference – if it exists. You normally need a *minimum* of half a dozen individual measurements in each sample.

SUMMARY

- Abiotic factors, including temperature, pH, light intensity and oxygen content, can often be conveniently monitored and recorded by means of electronic sensors and datalogging equipment.

- The species richness of a community is a measure of how many species are in the community.

- Random sampling is generally needed to determine the distribution and abundance of organisms, due to their uneven distribution.

- Quadrats, point quadrats and belt transects can all be employed to sample immobile organisms.

- Kite diagrams can be used to show the abundance and distribution of organisms in a belt transect.

- Measures of the abundance of organisms sampled by means of quadrats include species frequency, the density of individuals in a species and percentage cover.

- The capture–recapture technique can be used to assess the abundance of mobile organisms provided certain assumptions hold true.

- The plant species found in an area are greatly affected by the types of soil present.

- Soils can be analysed in terms of their particle size distribution, organic matter content, water content, air content, pH and nutrient content.

- The chi-squared test and t-test can be used to analyse ecological data and assign appropriate confidence levels to any conclusions drawn.

Questions

1 Describe how abiotic factors can be measured and assess their importance.

2 Describe the ways in which soils can be analysed.

3 Explain the circumstances in which you would use each of the following methods to determine the distribution and/or abundance of organisms:
   a 1 m × 1 m quadrats;
   b point quadrats;
   c capture–recapture technique.

Answers to self-assessment questions

Chapter 1

1.1 Ecosystem, community, habitat, microhabitat.

1.2 The organisms in the ecosystem.

1.3 91 250 000 (when there are 365 days in a year).

1.4 Levels: diversity of ecosystems (in a region), number of species (in each ecosystem), genetic diversity within (the populations of each) species. Scales: global, national, local.

Chapter 2

2.1 Both actions would be expected to decrease the numbers of grouse. More frequent burning would reduce the availability of old heather for shelter and nesting; less frequent burning would reduce the growth of young heather shoots for food.

2.2 Intercropping would usually be expected to work best when crops with different niches are grown as this would reduce competition between the two crops and allow them to use, at least to some extent, different resources.

2.3 a China has increased its fertiliser application the most as a result of increasing intensification of its farming to feed its growing population.
  b The Netherlands, with a stable population, has decreased its fertiliser application the most as the result of a recognition that its rate of use of fertiliser was unsustainable.

2.4 a Pesticide use may result in the loss of natural pest controls, such as parasites and predators.
  b Pests may evolve resistance to pesticides.

Chapter 3

3.1 Nutrient enrichment leads to a big increase in the numbers of aerobic bacteria, which leads to a fall in dissolved oxygen levels to below the point necessary for the survival of certain species. Blooms of algae or cyanobacteria may block light and so prevent plants from growing.

3.2 Biochemical oxygen demand provides a measure of the present extent of eutrophication. Indicator species provide a summary of the recent (typically over several months) history of water quality.

3.3 $(4 + 3 + 3 + 3 + 2) \div 5 = 3$

3.4 Five from: damage to trees (especially conifers); damage to lichens; damage to fish; damage to crustaceans; damage to molluscs; possible failure of some birds to breed.

3.5 CFCs release free radicals which break ozone, O_3, down to oxygen gas, O_2, thus leading to the thinning of the ozone layer. CFCs, along with other greenhouse gases, enhance the natural greenhouse effect of the atmosphere and so contribute to global warming.

Chapter 4

4.1 Four from: reduce fishing quotas; police fishing fleets to ensure quotas are observed; involve fishermen and scientists in the management; reduce bycatches/increase net size; encourage fish farming.

4.2 Five from: slopes unstable; low water retention; high rate of leaching; minerals required for plant growth in short supply; low pH; very low in organic matter.

4.3 Re-using means using items again in their original form. Recycling includes re-using but also includes breaking objects down and then re-forming them into useful articles, e.g. pulping down paper for manufacture into cardboard.

4.4 Yes, the repeated use of milk bottles is an instance of re-use.

Chapter 5

5.1 Three from: farming is permitted in them, forestry is permitted in them; quarrying/mining is permitted in them; pressure from tourists.

5.2 SSSIs are areas of particular scientific importance whose conservation relies on protection whereas ESAs are areas of national environmental significance whose conservation depends on particular farming methods.

5.3 2% (as the RSPB has just over 1 million members and there are about 60 million people in the UK).

Chapter 6

6.1 Mammals, especially large ones, rare ones or cute ones.

6.2 Small ones, inbred ones and endangered ones whose habitats are under pressure.

6.3 **a** 900/15 000 000 = 0.006%.
b 40 000/300 000 = 13%.

6.4 Four from: valuable products from elephants (ivory, meat, elephant hide); ethical – elephants have a right to live; aesthetic – elephants are magnificent, give pleasure to people; tourist income; role played by elephants in ecosystem.

6.5 Three from: year-round warmth; year-round moisture; trees are evergreen (so can photosynthesise all year); lots of plant species which between them fill many niches and so utilise nearly all the sunlight.

Chapter 7

7.1 30 %

7.2 Increasing the size of the quadrat used would increase the species frequency.

7.3 Estimate = 83 × 127/23 = 458.3. So, to the nearest 10, the best estimate is 460 woodmice.

7.4 (i) The population size will be underestimated;
(ii) The population size will be overestimated;
(iii) The population size will be overestimated;
(iv) The population size will be overestimated;
(v) The population size will be underestimated;
(vi) The population size will be overestimated;

7.5 Inorganic particles, minerals.

Glossary

abiotic factors	The physical characteristics of a habitat.	Include temperature, light intensity and pH.
acid rain	Rain acidified by oxides of sulphur and nitrogen released during the combustion of fossil fuels and metal smelting. Even unpolluted rain is weakly acidic (pH 5.6) due to dissolved carbon dioxide producing carbonic acid.	Also includes acidified mists and dry deposition.
biochemical oxygen demand (BOD)	The amount of oxygen used up by microorganisms in breaking down organic matter in a polluted water sample.	Units: milligrammes per cubic decimeter per 5 days $(\text{mg dm}^{-3}\ 5\ \text{day}^{-1})$. *See also* **eutrophication**
biodiversity	A measure of the biological richness of an area taking into account the number of species, community complexity and genetic variation within populations. Can be assessed at the local, national or global scale.	Shorthand for biological diversity.
biological pest control	The use of natural predators, parasites or disease organisms to control pests on field crops and in glasshouses.	Used as part of organic farming practice. *See also* **organic farming**
captive breeding	The breeding of rare or endangered animals in zoos, animal sanctuaries or wildlife parks with the aim of maintaining the species and its genetic diversity. The further aim is to increase numbers sufficiently for animals to be released back into wild habitats.	
capture–recapture technique	A method of determining population size involving catching and marking animals, releasing them back into their population and recatching individuals from the same population.	Includes use of the Lincoln Index.
chi-squared test	A statistical procedure used to determine whether observed numbers or ratios differ significantly from those expected.	$\text{Chi-squared} = \Sigma\ \dfrac{(O - E)^2}{E}$
conservation	Human activity to manage the resources of the Earth – includes preservation of habitats or species, management of ecosystems, reclamation of damaged habitats and even the creation of new ones.	*See also* **preservation**

deflected succession	Alteration of the natural changes in structure and species composition in a community due to the intervention of human activity. For example, burning, mowing or the use of grazing livestock reduce the vegetation to grassland and prevent natural succession to woodland.	Results in a plagioclimax community.
Environmentally Sensitive Area (ESA)	Area in the UK of national environmental significance where changes in farming methods pose a threat to the environment. A European Union prompted regulation where farmers can be funded to manage the land appropriately.	43 medium to large areas.
eutrophication	An increase in the nitrates, phosphates or organic content of aquatic systems. Pollution is the usual cause of eutrophication in lakes and rivers and is sometimes called anthropogenic or cultural eutrophication.	*See also* **biochemical oxygen demand**
extensive farming	Crop or livestock production from land with little or no fertiliser added (less than 20 kg per hectare per year). Yields are usually low.	*See also* **intensive farming**
global warming	The possible result of increasing greenhouse gases such as carbon dioxide, methane and halocarbons due to burning fossil fuels and other human activities. The consequences are still uncertain.	*See also* **greenhouse effect**
greenhouse effect	The trapping of the Sun's heat within the Earth's atmosphere. As many greenhouse gases are increasing due to human activities, the greenhouse effect may be getting stronger.	*See also* **global warming**
indicator species	Species which are sensitive to pollution in their habitat. Presence or absence of particular groups of such species indicates the level or type of pollution in the habitat.	Examples include lichens and freshwater invertebrates.
intensive farming	Crop or livestock production from land with more than 20 kg fertiliser per hectare per year. Yields vary from low to very high.	*See also* **extensive farming**
intercropping	Growing two or more complementary crops on the same land at the same time to maximise yields.	A traditional farming method.
kite diagram	Way of displaying the results of a belt transect.	The distribution of each species is represented as a 'diamond' shape where the width represents abundance and the length shows distribution along the transect.
National Park	Area of England or Wales of beautiful and relatively wild country where the characteristic landscape is preserved by law and where public access is provided while maintaining established farming methods.	11 large areas.

organic farming	Farming without using synthetic chemicals as fertilisers or pesticides. Modern organic farmers must register with a monitoring association and adhere to several regulations.	*See also* **biological pest control**
percentage cover	A measure of the relative abundance of plants or sessile animals in a community. Usually determined using quadrats; it can either be given as a number or as an abundance scale with about 5 categories.	Units: % or DAFOR or ACFOR or the Braun–Blanquet scale.
preservation	Human activity to avoid damage to, or destruction of particular habitats or ecosystems.	*See also* **conservation**
recycling	Recovery of material such as glass, paper or metals which would otherwise be thrown into landfill sites. Some items can be re-used; others are processed to make new products.	
seed bank	Collection of plant seeds preserved by freezing at low humidity to extend their normal period of viability. Both wild seed species and agricultural varieties can be stored.	Many tropical seeds cannot be stored frozen.
Site of Special Scientific Interest (SSSI)	Area in the UK of particular scientific importance relating to its flora, fauna, geology or appearance with statutory protection under the law. Called **Area of Special Scientific Interest** in Northern Ireland.	About 6500, usually small areas.
soil analysis	The experimental investigation of a soil to determine its different components: organic matter, air, water and particle size.	Nutrient availability and pH can also be investigated.
species frequency	A measure of the abundance and distribution of a species in a habitat. It equals the percentage of quadrats in which the species is found.	Units: % of quadrats (depends on size of quadrat).
species richness	At its simplest this is the number of species in a community. A more meaningful measure would specify the names of all the species and their classification into taxonomic groups.	
t-test	A statistical proceedure used to determine whether the means of two samples differ significantly.	$$t = \frac{\bar{x} - \bar{y}}{\sqrt{\frac{(s_x)^2}{n_x} + \frac{(s_y)^2}{n_y}}}$$

Index

Acknowledgements

Photographs

1.1 David T Grewcock/Frank Lane Picture Agency (FLPA); 1.2 S Maglowski/FLPA; 1.5 The Hutchison Library; 1.6 Lawson Wood/©Woodfall Wild Images; 2.1 E & D Hosking/FLPA; 2.2, 3.14 ©David Woodfall/Woodfall Wild Images; 2.3, 2.4 ©Mark Edwards/Still Pictures; 2.6 ©Ecoscene/Alan Towse; 2.8a Freedom Food, the RSPCA's farm animal welfare assurance labelling scheme; 2.8b Soil Association Certification Ltd; 2.9 Dr Jeremy Burgess/Science Photo Library; 3.1 ©Heather Angel/Natural Visions; 3.2 Emma Coleman/Environmental Images; 3.5 ©Chris Mattison/FLPA; 3.7 ©Ingrid Moorjohn/Still Pictures; 4.1 National Trust Photographic Library/David Levenson; 4.2 SimonFraser/Science Photo Library; 4.3 Jupiter Urban Wildlife Centre, Grangemouth. Scotland; 4.5 ©Bob Gibbs/Woodfall Wild Images; 4.7 R Roberts/Environmental Images; 5.1 W H Palmer/The Wildlife Trusts; 5.2 Steve Morgan/Environmental Images; 5.3 Bob Gibbons/Ardea London Ltd; 5.5 National Trust Photographic Library/Joe Cornish; 5.7,5.8 ©RSPB; 6.1 W Wisniewski/FLPA; 6.2 ©Doug Wechsler/BBC Natural History Unit; 6.3 Pete Addis/Environmental Images; 6.4 ©Diane Blell/Still Pictures; 6.5 ©Fred Hoogervorst/Foto Natura/FLPA; 6.7 ©Silvestris/FLPA; 6.8 NASA/Science Photo Library; 6.9 Pilley Cowell/Environmental Images; 7.1, 7.2 ©John Walmsley; 7.3 Andrew Cleave/Nature PhotographersLtd; 7.6 Brinsley Burbridge/Nature Photographers Ltd; 7.8 James King-Holmes/Science Photo Library

Picture Research: Maureen Cowdroy

Tables

2.1 from G. R. Miller and A. Watson, 1983, 'Heather moorland in Northern Britain', in A. Warren and F.B. Goldsmith (eds), *Conservation in Perspective*, 101–17, reprinted by permission of John Wiley & Sons Ltd; 2.2 data from The World Resources Institute *World Resources 1994–95* and *1998–99*, Oxford University Press Inc.; 2.3 from W. H. Dowdeswell, 1987, *Hedgerows and Verges*, Allen & Unwin imprint of HarperCollins Publishers Ltd; 3.1 data from MAFF, 1991, *Code of Good Agricultural Practice for the Protection of Water*, Crown Copyright; 3.2 from B. Moss, 1988, *Ecology of Fresh Waters: Man and Medium*, 2nd edn, Blackwell Science Ltd; 6.1 data from M. A. Houston, 1994, *Biological Diversity: Coexistence of Species*, Cambridge University Press; 7.3 , 7.4 adapted from J. H. Zar, 1984, *Biostatistical Analysis*, Prentice-Hall International

Diagrams

1.2 from Whittaker et al, 1973 ,'Niche, habitat and ecotope', in *American Naturalist* **107**, 321–38, University of Chicago Press; 1.3 data from E. S. Deevey, 1960, *Scientific American* **203** September 194–204; 1.4 data from I. G. Simmons, 1989, *Changing the face of the Earth*; 2.5 from L.T. Evans, 1975, *Crop Physiology: Some case histories*, Cambridge University Press; 2.10 from N. W. Moore, 1983, 'Ecological effects of pesticides', in A. Warren and F.B. Goldsmith (eds), *Conservation in Perspective*, 159–75, reprinted by permission of John Wiley & Sons Ltd; 3.3 from AGROW, 1995, 'Upturn in world agrochemical sales in 1994', in *World Protection News* **238** August 20; 3.4 from M. Rowland, 1992, *Biology*, Thomas Nelson & Sons Ltd; 3.8 from O. L. and Rose F. Hawksworth, 1976, *Lichens as Pollution Monitors*, reproduced by permission of Edward Arnold (Publishers) Ltd, London; 3.9 from J. C. Farman, British Antarctic Survey; 3.10 data from S Oberthur, 1997, 'Production and consumption of ozone-depleting substances 1986–95', in The World Resources Institute *World Resources 1998–99*, Oxford University Press Inc.; 3.11 from Professor C. D. Keeling, Scripp's Institution of Oceanography, US; 3.12 from A.M. Mannion, 1997, *Global environmental change*, 2nd edn, Addison Wesley Longman, New York; 3.13 partly from J. Gribbin, 1988, 'The greenhouse effect', in *New Scientist, Inside Science* **22** October 1–4; 6.5 from L. Cole, 1983, 'Urban nature conservation', in A. Warren and F. B. Goldsmith (eds), *Conservation in Perspective*, 267–85, reprinted by permission of John Wiley & Sons Ltd; 4.6 from G. E. Petts and I. Maddock, 1996, 'Flow allocation for in-river needs', in G. E. Petts and P. Calow (eds), *River Restoration*, Blackwell Science Ltd; 5.6 from MAFF, 1994, Crown Copyright; 7.4 adapted from G. Williams, 1987, *Techniques and Fieldwork in Ecology*, Bell & Hyman imprint of HarperCollins Publishers Ltd; 7.5 data from M. J Reiss; 7.7 from N. Chalmers and P. Parker, 1989, *The OU Project Guide: Fieldwork and Statistics for Ecological Projects*, Field Studies Council